DEPRESSION **doomed**

I can overcome it and achieve

the best version

of myself

MARIO F SALAZAR

MARIO SIN LIMITES
The Power of Introspection

www.mariosinlimites.com
https://humanintrospection.wixsite.com/website
mario.sinlimites@yahoo.com

PROLOGUE

Many years passed for the author of this book to find a satisfactory answer to his search.

His affliction for the ravages of depression, led him seeking help in different ways until, as a last resort he thought that perhaps God could.

He attended many churches where he thought God could look at and heal him. It took more than 10 years for him to realize that what he hoped for would not happen the way he had excitedly been told and motivated to continue praying God and for the miracle to happen.

And the miracle happened... not in the way he had been told but he discovered "A New God" and wrote a book with that same title to share the stumbles he found on his way to see the light.

In that book, he explained that God was not there as the genius of the wonder lamp to whom you can ask for 3 wishes and be fulfilled. God was not expecting someone to ask for a miracle to evaluate whether he deserves it or not.

And now in this new book he explains how that New God "inspired" him to understand what it is

*"depression" why it happens and what can be done
to overcome the havoc it causes in those to whom it
manages to subdue.*

*That's why, besides that he invites you to know the
true meaning of God and to practice a religion...
He developed a seminar-workshop whose goal is to
help those who are suffering because of this popular
"mental illness"... depression.*

Sam

DEDICATION

*On this occasion, I very much want to dedicate this book to those millions of people who currently suffer from some of these so-called "mental illnesses", or "personality disorders" which should better be known as **"personal tribulations"** mainly caused by the imbalance and social inequality.*

To those people who are living in the hope that someone will help them enjoy the harmony of life, but who have not understood that disinformation is their main enemy.

To my dear children Bianca Sofia and Luis Mario who have witnessed the effort I have made to try to be a good father despite the impediments generated by the famous "mental illness" called depression.

To you who have seen me mourn due to the helplessness of not knowing how to defeat that enemy but despite of everything I have never stopped fighting... and thanks to this I have finally come to the conviction that the solution is inside me, if from the bottom of my heart and not only in appearance I am able to reach the renewing of my mind.

Thank you, children, for being close to me, for having confidence and for showing me your love... You know I really love you.

While I am alive I will not rest until the research I have been carryng out generates good fruits that will be shared with all those who suffer the same.

Finally, to my friends, family and all the people who listened to me and gave me their sincere opinion contributing to a"grain of sand" so that I could achieve this goal.

To all of them... a thousand thanks.

CONTENTS

Item 1

Legend of the "Phoenix Bird"

Having finished writing this project, and after thinking that maybe I hadn't found the right words to describe what had happened in my life and because I had come this far, I was lucky enough to meet the legend of the phoenix and me could see that it speaks just about the battle in which I had been immersed for many years fighting blindly trying to win.

Moreover, at the end of this project I had decided that this would be my last job, my last effort to defeat the enemy that always had me subdued... "depression" (a mental illness?).

I had decided that if nothing changed after this last attempt, then I would no longer do anything to defend myself... I was willing to abandon myself to my fate, I was willing to allow myself to be overwhelmed by fate. I was willing to put my knees on the ground and lower my head so that the executioner would wield his sword high and fulfill his mission. was willing to die even without understanding why.

But knowing that according to legend, the phoenix had been a victim destroyed by the fire of justice, and that then he was reborn from among his ashes demonstrating with this that by the will of God, adversity can be overcome, then I felt encouraged to think that I could also defeat my enemies and continue in my efforts to help others do so as well.

The Phoenix Bird expresses the resurrection, as well as immortality and the fight for overcoming. The Phoenix Bird is a warrior, an icon of inspiration.

(Source: Legend (https://biografía.org/ave-Fenix/)
The first references to the myth of the Phoenix are found in Ancient Egypt. Later, his account appeared in Ancient Greece in the works of Hesiod and Herodotus.

From the passage of time, history has adapted to different cultural and religious traditions.

Today the legend of the Phoenix is a source of inspiration to face new challenges after a bitter defeat.

It is a universal symbol that can be related to immortality, resurrection, or the ability to overlap adversity.

According to the Christian version of this legend the Phoenix Bird was born in Eden, under the Tree of

Good and Evil and next to a bush of roses. It stood out for its beautiful plumage and its beautiful singing.

Apart from its beauty, it had noble principles and for this reason, was the only being who did not want to try the forbidden fruits of the sacred tree.

Thus, when Adam and Eve were driven from Eden a spark of the sword of fire of a cherub and thus the bird burned immediately and ended up destroyed.

However, from his own ashes, he was reborn again with the same plumage and matchless singing. Immortality was the gift he received for his faithfulness to the divine command.

He/She was also rewarded with three great qualities: true knowledge, the healing capacity of her tears, and incredible strength.

In ancient Egyptian mythology, the Phoenix is a bird known as "Bennu", a bird symbolizing the floods of the Nile River. Ancient Greeks called the Phoenix "Phoenicoperos", which literally means red wings.

In the Christian tradition, the account of the Phoenix is symbolizing the resurrection of Christ and, in parallel, the destructive fire represents the idea of purification. In Mexican culture, the image of the Phoenix often appears associated with the God Quetzalcoatl.

The city of Phoenix is the capital of the state of Arizona and its name and flag are inspired precisely by the mythological narrative.

In today's psychology, the legend of the bird that was reborn from its own ashes is used to remember the importance of resilience, that is, the ability to overcome adversity and face any kind of personal challenge.

All people experience failure and disappointment at some point in their lives.

In this situation there are two possible strategies: to fall into defeatism and regrets or, on the contrary, to start a new course with more strength and determination.

The myth of the Phoenix Bird reminds us that no defeat is definitive and that within us we have the strength **to reinvent ourselves** and to start new projects.

Although the reference to the phoenix (also known as the firebird) does not appear by name in the biblical translation of the KJV, it does appear in a Jewish translation of the Old Testament.

It also appears in the Septuagint (a Greek version of the Old Testament dated in the 3rd century BC), Vulgate (The Latin version of Scripture compiled by Jerome in the 4th century), and some biblical commentary for Job 29:18.

The Hebrew word "khole" (Strong's Concordance #H2344), translated as 'sand' in the KJV, is interpreted as a reference to the phoenix in the Bible of the Society of Jewish Publications and other sources.

Then I said, 'I will die with my nest, and multiply my days as a phoenix;' (Job 29:18, Jewish Publication Society Bible of 1917)

Then I thought: with my nest, I will expire, and like the phoenix, have a long life (Keil and Delitzsch Commentary). Keil and Delitzsch's commentary justifies their translation of the phoenix (bird) in Job 29:18 as follows: "That this bird is none other than the phoenix, it is put beyond doubt by the Midrashim (collected in the Jalkut on Job, 517)...

On the contrary, we must immediately welcome a reference to the Egyptian-Egyptian-Egyptian myth of the Phoenix, which can be tested in a book that also thoroughly mixes Egyptian things with Arabs... (Commentary by Keil and Delitzsch, comments on Job 29: 18 –

Item 2

Introduction

We all know that "physical" diseases, even for a short period of time, can prevent us from doing our daily activities and that once restored, usually everything is back to the way it was.

However, "mental" illnesses have not been controlled by science and it is unclear whether the patient can be restored, or how long could it take or never able to be "normal" again.

Therefore, this work, like the intention of my book "A New God", is intended to help people suffering from some of the most famous "mental illnesses" of the last 100 years such as stress, anxiety, depression, etc., to know the origin of their "evil" disease and to discover and convince themselves if there can be any true way to heal.

In my book "A New God" it seems that the intention is to speak of God from a religious point of view, however by reading it carefully, you can notice that its purpose is to explain how faith in God well understood, can give us the power to heal our body and our soul.

The real message of this book is to share the results I found as I look for a way to heal my body and mind and how after trying in many ways and not getting it, as the last option, I thought God could help me.

And the most relevant thing is to say that didn't happen, I didn't get the help that I expected to find in God. but I must make CLEAR that it is not that God did not want or could help me, but that I did not know what or who is God or how to find it.

All I knew about God was what I had known through the films where Jesus ended up in the crucifixion. Films in which they projected a Jesus scolding many and performing miracles to those who crossed his path and were suffering or those who approached him to ask him.

To that God is the one I wanted to find, that God whose image appeared in all the Catholic churches and who I believed would also do me the miracle of healing as soon as I asked.

In that attempt, I discovered that this God that we came to confuse with the genius of the wonder lamp that could grant us up to 3 wishes… doesn't exist.

I discovered then that in the churches it is where we learn to believe that that kind of God does exist and that there in the church is where we can find him and if we ask him in faith he will heal us, so I did, I asked him in faith, but after many years passed and I did not stop suffering, I began to wonder why does

God was taken so long to help me? If I was not worthy of him? Or maybe there was something I was doing wrong.

In all the attempts I made without having the answer I expected, I always received words of "encouragement" telling me to be patient, that God knew what I was doing, and do not to stop praying.

I thought that nothing happened, I was desperate because I felt that no one knew how to explain to me what was happening and I no longer trusted anyone, so I continued to research on my own while still attending classes, seminars, and workshops offered by the churches where they promise that those who are suffering will find relief and the answer we were seeking.

I came to think that maybe I was in the wrong church because I started to go to Christian churches when I had grown up within the Catholic church. I came to think that maybe that would be the reason and then I also tried to return to Catholicism and for this, I took a catechism course for about 9 months, until I realized that I was also not getting the help I was looking for. and so I began to visit not only other Christian churches but of another kind in order to find it wherever God might be.

Until there came a time when I began to suspect that something was wrong with what the churches taught me or that maybe I was the one doing something wrong. and from that moment on I began to write down everything I had tried, including all the courses and classes I had participated in with that single goal of being healed.

In virtually all large churches, courses are given that to a greater or lesser extent offer that you will know God intimately and that you will learn to ask Him to heal you. and that he will.

I do not complain about the good intention of the churches, but although I know that they put all their efforts, it is not one of their primary activities, so they do not devote enough time to achieve that object and usually the course or class only end up being an informative talk that sometimes motivates.

Then, the present work aims to expand and explain in more detail how faith in God can work so that we can help ourselves in the recovery of our health.

The result of this work will lead you to know how you can achieve the best version of yourself and how to feel in harmony in the world in which you live.

Item 3

Background

Until these moments in my life (mid-2019) and having participated, studied and compared various techniques, methods and treatments offered by the mental or spiritual health market, I have come to understand that my body and mind have not been sick but that have only reflected the consequences of the unfavorable circumstances that have been part of my life… So from now on, I will no longer be a "mentally ill", but only a "person with tribulations"

In essence, what I just said is how those circumstances make us "abnormal" and that abnormality is what doctors, psychologists, and psychiatrists have called "mental illness."

In my case, depression limits me to being the person I think could be if I were "normal"... Depression to me is like "a wet, slippery dark cage that squeezes me and makes my breathing difficult, fills me with fear and anguish, and immobilizes me while causing great dislike in others"

Looking closely at a series of events, I could see that since I was born there were situations that caused me emotional suffering even if in those moments I did not have the ability to recognize it, I did not even know if I was sad, frightened, distressed or anxious.

As I grew older, the anguish and fear experienced from my earliest childhood manifested themselves without me being able to avoid it or understand it, I know because now in the distance in time, I remember myself as a restless and naughty child but at the same time introverted and anxious mainly when I was not accompanied either by friends or family.

As an adult, I realized that as a child I had started to have some of the characteristic symptoms of depression, but no one noticed or did not know what to do with me and therefore never received help so I grew up in the midst of a lot of inner pain.

When I was able to take care of myself, I started looking for help where I was supposed to and where surely we would all do according to what we learned from childhood, that is, we all know that if we are sick we should visit the doctor.

I did it and I didn't find the solution, then I visited the psychologist and then the psychiatrist and "the witch" and other types of healers and after many years of searching it was the same or worse because the suffering I lived continued to grow by not receiving the proper treatment.

Much of the bad that I went living at different stages of my life, was accumulating negatively and as I grew up I did not find something that I could be proud of, rather I considered myself as someone whom many rejected, I felt afraid to participate socially because I did not know how to behave and was not able to be part of any group and I arrive at the time where my only relief was alcohol and at any social event I only dedicated myself to drinking and doing it in excess.

By the time I finished my professional studies and perhaps since much earlier, I had already lost the sense of what was right, I had already broken many rules that the community could consider sacred and even my own family began to avoid my presence when I abused alcohol for saying offensive words and provoked the anguish of those around me.

After the effects of alcohol, I realized my defiances and shame and repentance came, and worst of all, I often didn't even remember what I had done or said and sometimes neither where I had been nor with whom.

Living in this way no one can be considered "normal", yet I wanted those who saw my misfortune to think what I thought of myself, that I was suffering from many deficiencies and that I was a victim of mistreating and abandonment. but of course, no one cared more about me, all they cared about was that I would be close to them again.

DEPRESSION **doomed**

With all that background and previous experiences, I became involved in several sentimental relationships, some inconsequential and others of great importance and now I know that a man like me in those times, was not able to form a relationship of respect and responsibility, so virtually none of the relationships I had could end up in a happy ending.

I didn't feel sick but I was living the most painful consequences of my misfortune whether provoked by myself, inherited or learned without realizing it.
I had become irritable and suspicious, my self-esteem was almost zero, I felt sorry for myself, and I wanted no one to notice.

I could never tell if someone intentionally attacked my feelings and convictions, or whether it was just a predisposition on my part.

Something that excelled in my introspection, was that in the midst of so much misery there was a season where everything became joy, motivation, desire to live and to succeed...

Those moments happened when love first came into my life, I fell in love with a girl I dreamed I would live happily. and I'm sure that's how it would have been if the demons that dwelled within me had remained chained.

Then, and because in spite of everything I am still alive, it is easy to realize that even in the midst of the most difficult conditions, thanks to God's grace, the human being can get ahead, change his suffering for joy if he finds a motivator strong enough and important enough. and that motivator can be the company of a person to whom you can trust the secrets of your heart and without being judged or sentenced, it gives you understanding and holds your hand without cheating or lying.

Or, the motivator may be the one that each person needs, for example, the acknowledge to his work, social acceptance, and the main one that is healthy.

So it would do us a lot of good to learn or develop our ability to socialize to live with the community where surely someone will have to be waiting for you, to give you what you need, and for that, we need to know each other, learn to forgive and to close old wounds.

Item 4

Same language

Miscommunication and misinterpretation of the law are the fundamental reasons for misuse of language because even though we all speak the same language, we do not all understand the meaning of many words even though they are already defined in dictionaries.

This means that often a person can use words as if he truly understood their meaning and then assumes that what others heard or say is understandable equally.

That's why and to help the purpose of this book, and according to the dictionary definition, we'll review some words that we should all know and understand the same meaning to make sure we're speaking the "same language."

Anguish: Affliction, grief, anxiety. / Oppressive fear without precise cause. / Suffocation, sensation of oppression in the thoracic or abdominal region...

Anxiety: A state of agitation, restlessness or worries that usually goes with many diseases, in particular, certain neuroses, and which does not allow the sick to calm down.

Bipolar: It is a manic-depressive mental disorder, which causes a lot of unhappiness to carriers of this disease, despite being a mental illness with simple treatment. Bipolar disorder is characterized by two phases: the manic phase and the depressive phase.

The two phases are distinguished by different symptoms. Although the symptoms of the two phases can co-exist in what is known as a mixed period.

Catharsis: Catharsis is a purifying experience of human emotions. As such, the word comes from the Greek (kátharsis), which means 'purge', 'purification'. The words cleanliness or release can be used as synonyms for catharsis.

In the area of Psychology, catharsis is a method by which, during the therapy process, a patient is led to unlocking memories or experiences repressed in his unconscious, usually associated with traumatic events of the past, with the aim of to be able to talk about it, raise awareness, and experience it emotionally

Christ: In Christian theology, the Son of God, made man, "The anointed" The word "anointed" is the Spanish translation of the word "Messiah" in English, and the definition of "MESSIAH" according to the dictionary is: "The King that the Jews expected to come".

This word began to be used in the year 1560 and literally, means "anointed" in English "anointed".

Anointed: King or priest signified with the holy oil; Anoint. Choosing someone for a position or for a position

Conscious: Who feels, thinks, wants and works with knowledge of what he does. With full use of the senses and faculties.

Death: Cessation or end of life, separation of body and soul.

Destination: Hado (unknown force believed to work on men and events)

Devil: In the Judeo-Christian tradition, each of the angels rebelled against God and cast by Him into the abyss; the prince of those angels who represent the spirit of evil.

Dogma: The word comes from the Latin dogmaticus, and this in turn from the Greek "dogmatikós", and is derived from "dogma", which means 'thought', 'principle', 'doctrine'.

In a derogatory sense, a person or institution that is uncompromising, and whose ideas and opinions are objectionable is called dogmatic: "Reason, don't be so dogmatic."

In matters of religion, dogmatic theology is one that studies the theoretical principles upon which faith in God and his works is based, as it is preached and instructed by the Church, from which considerations in a moral sense around the truth and significance of his teachings.

Essence: What constitutes the nature of things, the permanent and unchanging of them. The most important and characteristic of one thing.

Faith: A set of beliefs of someone, a group, or a multitude of people. Confidence, a good concept you have of someone or something...
One of the most painful ways to obtain faith is after experiencing "the ultimate expression of desolation"

Genetics: Belonging to or relating to the genesis or origin of things. Part of the biology that deals with inheritance and its related.

Fantasy: Top degree of imagination; imagination as soon as it invents or produces.

Forgiveness: Remission of the worthly deserved, Indulgence (remission of sins).

Free will: Faculty, ability to act according to one's will or choice, example: leave him to his free will and discover the boundary between good and evil / Way to act according to whim or whim /   Freely, without any support, example: to his agency will know to choose the best solution.

God: To be supremely considered a doer of the universe. According to what the scholars wrote in the dictionary, this is how everyone should accept the definition of God. "To be supreme" "Maker of the universe".

The word "to be" is defined as Essence or nature. And the expression Being supreme is defined as God.

Habit: Special way of proceeding or conducting acquired by repetition of equal or similar acts, or originated by intuitive tendencies. The situation of dependence on certain drugs.

Heaven: In the Christian tradition, the dwelling place in which angels, saints and the blessed enjoy the presence of God

Hell: Definitive deprivation of God. Place where the condemned suffer eternal punishment after death. Place where there is much uproar, discord or violence, and destruction.

Hope: State of the mood in which what we want is presented to us as possible. In Christian doctrine, theological virtue for which God is expected to give the goods he has promised.

Idea: It is the mental representation of something that may be related to the real or imaginary world. This word comes from the Greek "eidos" meaning "I saw".

Illness: It comes from the Latin "infirmitas" which means "Lack of firmness", is the more or less serious change in the health of a living being.

This alteration or condition of an individual's health may be of a physical, mental or social type, i.e. a person may be sick if he has suffered any loss of health in the physical (body), mental (psyche or brain) and/or social (by the community)

Imagination: Faculty of the soul that represents images of real or ideal things. False apprehension or judgment of something that is not really or unfounded

Imagine: Ideally, represent something, invent it, create it in the imagination. Believing or pretending to be something. Show off, suspect.

Ineffable: The ineffable term is a qualifying adjective, which refers to those situations or things that by its excellent qualities cannot be expressed in words.

The ineffable cannot be described through language, whether by being sublime, by subtle or original.

Inspire: God's Saying: Enlighten someone's understanding and move their will. Infuse or give birth in the spirit or mind, affections, ideas, designs, etc.

DEPRESSION **doomed**

Intellect: Understanding, rational cognitive power of the human soul.

Introspection: Inner look that is directed to one's own acts or moods.

Intuition: Feeling, ability to understand things instantly, without the need for reasoning.

Language: Articulated sounds with which man manifests what he thinks or feels. Set of signals that hint at something

Lie: Saying or manifesting the opposite of what is known, believes or thinks. pretend/ fake something.

Life: Union of soul and body. Substantial internal force or activity, through which the being who possesses it works.

Madness: It is an extreme irrational state according to the parameters of a given culture or society.

Madness is synonymous with foolishness, and sometimes genius.

Today, madness has both a positive and negative connotation even though its origin goes back to the reference of a mentally ill person or who rejected the common sense of the time.

In psychological terms, insanity is not a disorder or mental illness such as psychosis, schizophrenia, paranoia and bipolar disorder.

Meditate: Apply thought with deep attention to consideration of something, or go about the means of knowing or getting it.

Mind: Intellectual power of the soul. Set of conscious and unconscious psychic activities and processes, especially cognitive in nature.

Miracle: Rare, extraordinary and wonderful event or thing. A fact not explained by natural laws and attributed to supernatural intervention of divine origin.

I would add that a miracle is something that could happen or not, could be good or evil but never thought as possible something extremely unexpected.

Parable: Narration of a fake event that an important truth or moral teaching is inferred by comparison or likeness.

Personality: Individual difference that constitutes each person and distinguishes it from another / Set of original features or qualities that stand out in some people/ Set of qualities that constitute the person or intelligent subject.

Religion: A set of beliefs or dogmas about divinity, feelings of veneration and fear towards it, of moral norms for individual and social conduct, and of ritual practices, mainly prayer and sacrifice to worship him.

Sacred: Worthy of veneration and respect for its divine character or for being related to divinity. Unmodifiable. Their customs are sacred, something superhuman

Sin: Which departs from the right and just, or that lacks what is due. Conscious transgression of a religious precept.

Soul: In some religions and cultures, the spiritual and immortal substance of human beings, that which gives spirit, encouragement, and strength to something.

Spirit: To be immaterial and endowed with reason. Generator principle, intimate character, essence or substance of something, animated, courage, encouragement, verve, effort.

Stress: Tension caused by overwhelming situations that cause psychosomatic reactions or sometimes severe psychological disorders.

Subconscious: Something that does not become conscious. It refers to the subconscious or inferior state of psychological consciousness in which, because of the low intensity or duration of perceptions, the individual does not realize them.

Thinking: Reflect, carefully examine something to form an opinion. Imagine, consider or run.

Thought: Thought is the faculty, action, and effect of thinking. The thought is also an idea or mental representation about something or someone perceived through the senses.

It is also understood as the ability to build ideas and concepts and to establish relationships between them.

It is also used to refer to an imaginary space of the mind where ideas are created and stored.
The thought is also a purpose or intention to accomplish something.

Therapy: Treatment of a disease or any dysfunction... treatment aimed at solving psychological problems.

Tribulation: Grief, grief, torment or moral affliction. / Persecution or adversity of a person.

Truth: Property of one thing to always keep it without any mutation. Clear expression, without batter or flattery, with someone being corrected or reprimanded. Reality (actual existence of something)

Verb: Sound or sounds, words that express an idea that can vary from person, number, time, mode and appearance. The second person of the Holy Trinity.

Will: Faculty to decide and order one's conduct. Intention, encouragement or resolve to do something. Free will or self-determination. Choice of something without precept or external impulse that obliges it.

This word seems to indicate that we have the power to do or no to do something but what we choose, we want and allow. But the reality seems to be different if not, go to Rom 7: 15 "Because what I do, I don't understand; because I don't do what I want, but what I hate, that's what I do."
We'll also let's review some phrases or expressions like:

Speak figuratively:
As such, the figurative meaning is established based on the likeness of a word with an idea, concept, or feeling. That is, in figurative language, a word expresses an idea using another with which it bears a certain analogy, whether real or imaginary

Words, in this sense, have a connotative value, this means that their meaning can be extended or altered depending on the context or situation in which they are used. This can be seen, for example, in the following sentence: "Antonio is a tomb, he will never sing." In it, there are two terms used figuratively.

The first, "tomb", alludes to Antonio's ability or decision to shut up in an absolute and definitive way. The second, "singing," refers to the idea of confessing or delating. Because of the context and the situation that suggests the combination of the two words, we can then determine that they relate to a situation where someone who knows a secret and is determined to keep it to the end.

Examples of figurative phrases

- Rocío put a "wall" between us.
- I die for fear.
- That office is a "viper's nest."
- I fell asleep "like a stone in well".
- He's not a donkey, but he's "bouting."
- I've called you a thousand and three hundred times.

Mental illness:
Mental illnesses are serious conditions that can affect human thinking and people's actions. That's why when you talk about a person who doesn't have mental health, you might be in the presence of a person who has an illness or psychiatric problem.

This is also how the term mental health or hygiene is now associated with those activities aimed at achieving that necessary balance in people in their day-to-day life, such as exercising after a strong day's work, going to a retreat away or the city to enjoy the silence and nature, as well as the well-deserved vacation after a year of work, or an anti-stress or relaxation massage, all those activities seek to improve the health or mental hygiene of the individual to maintain that balance necessary in their daily lives.

DEPRESSION **doomed**

Mental health is associated with a person's reason, emotions and how they are controlled and outsourced, as well as their behavior in the face of the facts of daily life such as paying bills, losing their jobs, changing residences, etc. Mental health leads us to have a positive image of ourselves, so by having a good image of myself, I can project a good image to others.

The National Alliance Against Mental Illness (NAMI) says: Mental illness is a condition that affects a person's thinking, feeling, or mood. Such conditions can affect someone's ability to relate to others and function every day. Each person will have different experiences, even people with the same diagnosis.

Recovery, including significant roles in social life, school, and work, is possible, especially when you start treatment early and play an important role in your own recovery process.

A mental health condition is not the result of an event. Research suggests multiple causes of linking. Genetics, the environment and lifestyle influence whether someone develops a mental health condition.

Stressful work or home life make some people more susceptible, as do the traumatic events of life such as being a victim of a crime. Biochemical processes and circuits and basic brain structures can also play a role.

Free will:
Free will is the power that human beings have to act as they choose. This means that people naturally have the freedom to make their own decisions, without being subject to pressures, needs or limitations, or divine predetermination.

Free will means, in short, that human beings have the freedom both to do good and to do evil. And this, of course, has its ethical and moral implications, for the individual acting according to his free will is also responsible for his actions, whether they count or succeed or their mistakes.

Hence free will extends to other areas of human life, such as religion, philosophy or law.

Genetic inheritance:
The study of genetics allows understanding what happens in the cell cycle and how between humans are transferred biological characteristics (genotype), physical characteristics (phenotype) and even the personality itself, for example, "the great resemblance between the parents and their descendants." In reference to the indicated, the cell cycle is the process by which the cell grows and is divided into two daughter cells.

The transfer of the characteristics of a being is developed by genes, composed of DNA (Deoxyribonucleic acid) which is a molecule that encodes genetic data in cells, stores and transmits from generation to generation information necessary for the progress of all biological functions of an organism.

Psychosomatic diseases:
Diseases related to psychosomatic disorders include hypertension, asthma, flu, cancer, impotence, allergies, cystitis, gastritis, diarrhea, anemia, among others.

A person may develop a psychosomatic disorder due to stress, a sedentary lifestyle, poor diet, consumption of certain substances harmful to health, among other factors that generate anxiety, distress, depression or concern. Social or cultural factors may also be associated with psychosomatic conditions.

All right, now we have a broader and clearer idea of words and phrases of great use, that will help us to understand and get fully into the fundamental objective of this book, which is:

"Helping people who suffer from
physical, emotional or social pain
to find the best way
to alleviate their grief,
to recover or learn to cope
to live with dignity, and to know
what they can do to become
the best version of themselves"

Item 5

What is mind

For a better understanding, I want to highlight and abound a little more about one of the keywords of this project:

The mind:

This is a word that most of us use in an imprecise way because we do not catch exactly what is the mind... some think that there are the thoughts derived from a process performed by the brain without us being able to prevent it, others think that they are the internal networks of the brain itself, others that it is the spirit or the soul.

From a grammatical, spelling or literal point of view, the word mind is described in dictionaries as:

"The intellectual power of the soul. Set of psychic activities and processes, conscious and unconscious, especially cognitive in nature."

I am sure that most of us do not refer to all this statement when we colloquially mention it.
Now, from a scientific point of view, the mind understands a person's set of intellectual abilities, such as perception, thought, consciousness, and memory.

It is also part of the human being where these processes develop.

The mind is also synonymous with thought, purpose or will. For example: "Arthur had his mindset on his marriage.

In Psychology, the concept of mind comprises the set of activities and processes, both conscious and unconscious, of a psychic character (psychic to the soul), such as perception, reasoning, learning, creativity, imagination or memory.

The mind is what allows us to have subjective consciousness.

As such, it does not occupy a physical place, hence it is an abstract concept.

It is usually associated with the brain, which is the organ in which these processes take place, but differs from this, while the mind is studied by disciplines such as psychology and psychiatry, the brain is approached from biology based on the physical and chemical process that takes place in it.

Dr. Caroline Leaf (Cognitive Neuroscientist) in her book "Turn Your Brain On" referring to scientific studies that have been done, explains it extensively, but in a very summed form, says:

1. The mind is what the brain does, indicating that it is the place where the chemical processes that create the mind are performed.

2. The brain is what the mind does, indicating that the thoughts and decisions we make, generate a genetic expression that is given in the brain.

3. In the spirit, there is intuition, communion, and consciousness

4. *The soul that at the same time is the* mind is responsible for intellect, emotions and free will

5. The body is only the physical part, the substance that can be seen

A. J. Miller (Master of Divine Truth) in Brisbane, Australia, through one of his videos on his page www.divenetruth.com explains (here only in a very short way) that:

1. The brain is part of our physical body and that in it is also the spiritual body and that everything is alive through the soul.

2. In the spiritual body is the mind-controlled by a higher power that leads us to generate correct thoughts.

3. The brain is located in the physical body and it perceives the existence of its being, that is, it handles basic information, collects information, stores it, compares it, discerns it and sends signals to the whole body so that its movement takes place.

As you can see, even those who have devoted a large part of their lives to handling these kinds of concepts, do not find it easy to explain clearly what we would like to know, so after reviewing these two authors and some others, I could realize that some of this concepts can be used interchangeably.

The point for us must be to understand their message to know how we are affected by what is called, mind, brain, soul or spirit.

With the information collected and clarifying that for some the words soul and spirit are synonymous, I think for our purpose, I would express it this way:

Soul: The divine spark, the energy that gives life.

Spirit: The "implant" made by God in our hearts containing information that guides our acts and actions according to his will (Spiritual Body – Holy Spirit)

Mind: The action that occurs simultaneously by the interaction of the spirit with the stimuli received (information) from the outside through our 5 senses, making decisions that materialize in thoughts that in turn the brain interprets, classifies, organizes and provokes reactions

Brain: A physical part of the body that synchronizes movements, actions, and reactions of physical, emotional or spiritual nature.

Then, to me, the human being is the body that we all can see, but we must understand and accept that the human being is not only his physical part, because it is enough to ask us, how does the body move, how it moves from one side to another , how do you listen, talk, reason and make decisions? And why isn't all that possible for animals or vegetables?

In my search for information, I have come to understand that the body moves with the impulse of the soul which is nothing but life itself, the "divine spark", that is, the presence of God our creator.

I've also concluded that the brain is like a computer, although of course, it's much more than that, but I make the computer analogy because that way it can be easier for us to understand than the brain, as long as it's just a material part without any will not perform any functions or tasks.

Almost everyone knows and understands that to use a computer it is necessary that in addition to the electrical energy has at least one basic program that allows it to start working, and later through different programs (instructions) that perform programmer engineers, we can make computers perform the tasks we want and function in optimal conditions as long as they are maintained and updated to make them more efficient, and it seems that today, we do not know how far they can evolve.

The brain is somehow like the computer that "manufactures" comes with basic information contained in what scientists call "reptilian brain" for it to perform basic functions or survival instincts.

Since the inert body (including the brain) receives the "divine spark" and the "spirit" reacts, it is already able to begin to receive more information, that is, it can either be "programmed" or "reprogrammed" with mental implants that will gradually go receiving throughout his life.

In this case, our parents and closest relatives are our primary "programmers", who are providing us with the most basic information to begin to perform increasingly complicated functions, such as learning to sit, stand and walk, take objects with your hands, knowing colors, smells and flavors... Etcetera.

Already in a later stage and with the new programmers that we will know (school, work, friends) we learn, reason, compare, discern and conclude. In a much more advanced stage, you learn to be creative.

In general, this is how we can understand in psychological terms the evolution of the human being from birth to death. And then here we can ask ourselves how and when **the suffering begins**?

Finally, we must hold in mind that the information that we are receiving and that I call "mental implants" is stored in our brain, which for me, is divided into at least 2 large "drawers"... conscious and subconscious.

Since a person starts to perceive the world around, he/she gives a sense or meaning according to the information he has received since childhood and that manifests itself through the interpretation of what he lives. that is, every situation or event is observed, analyzed, compared and discerned... that is, the process of thought is carried out and depending on its conclusions, the brain reacts by creating emotions that determine the feelings and actions of the person.

See the example on the following page

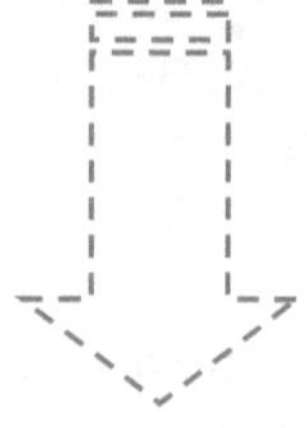

DEPRESSION **doomed**

Message received by the brain	Probably feeling	Person's reaction
I'm not good enough or I don't feel able	Emptiness in the stomach	I'd like someone to assure me that it's okay, that yes, I can
I'm a bad person	Chest tightness	I'd like to be alone, not see anyone
I should have listened to my friend and not argued with him	The heart beats very fast	Apologize over and over again even if the friend tells you that everything is fine
I'm very stressed, I need to stop thinking	Too overwhelmed	Drinking alcohol or using drugs to escape
They're not going to hire me for this job.	Stumping, fear	Try to find a justification for not going to the interview
I'm not going to get my exposure right.	A little drowsy, a little dizzy	I'd like to find someone to replace me or postpone
He/She is going to leave me	Fear, nervousness, butterflies in the stomach	Check the email waiting for him/ her to say everything is ok.
I'm very angry with her, but she's to blame.	Heat in the face and arms	Arguing and arguing even though she's not to blame
I really want to eat something sweet.	Salivation, hunger	Eating ice cream or chocolates even if I'm trying to lose weight
I want to eat bacon, although cholesterol can make me sick	The urgency to please a craving	Running the risk of cholesterol rising and damaging cholesterol

These, like other brain reactions generated by our thoughts, are those that can contribute to the development of **psychosomatic diseases**.

Example of False Thoughts	Likely Consequences
<ul><li>I'm crazy, I'm sick</li><li>I would like to be as good as...</li><li>Nobody cares about me.</li><li>They're going to turn me down.</li><li>Something's wrong with me.</li><li>Looks like everybody else is fine.</li><li>I have no control or will.</li><li>No one notices me, maybe he's always alone</li><li>I can't even take care of myself, or others.</li><li>Maybe he deserves to suffer.</li><li>I have habits I can't change</li><li>Sometimes I wish I was dead</li><ul><li>Etcetera.</li></ul></ul>	<ul><li>I'm always tired</li><li>Anxiety</li><li>Anguish</li><li>Fear</li><li>Excessive anger</li><li>Hate</li><li>Sweating</li><li>Tachycardias</li><li>Pain in the chest, back, arms</li><li>Vomiting wins</li><li>Sadness, depression, fatigue</li><li>A lot of sleep</li><li>Swollen body</li><li>Diabetes</li><li>Infarcts</li><ul><li>Etcetera.</li></ul></ul>

All this happens invisibly due to the process of the mind that induces generating thoughts that affect the functions of the brain and that are reflected in our personality, our social relationships and our physical and emotional health.

That is why it is too important that we have understood what it is THE MIND and how it acts in our being, for only in this way we will be able to understand how to change it or put it otherwise, how to change our way of thinking according to the sacred book in Rom 12: 2 "... Do not conform to the world today, but be transformed by renewing your mind. So you can see what God's will is, good, pleasant and perfect."

Note that Rom 12:2 says that only if you renew your mind you will realize how good and great God's will is, that if you don't stop thinking and acting like you've been letting yourself be taken away by what everyone says, then you will not be able to understand his will and you will not have access to his kingdom.

Changing the way you think or renew your mind is the same as "reborn."
In John 3:3, Jesus tells Nicodemus "... Verily, verily, I say unto you, that he who is not born again cannot see the kingdom of God." ...

And by way of clarification in John 3:5-7 it says, "Indeed, indeed, I say unto you, that he that is not born of water and of the spirit cannot enter into the kingdom of God. What is born of the flesh, the flesh is; and what is born of the Spirit, the spirit is. Don't marvel at me that I told you: You need to be born again.

Jesus is talking about two types of birth, the first is the "carnal" birth and the second one he refers to is the "spiritual" birth.

Being born of water means "being baptized" in the name of Jesus is the personal declaration of accepting Him as one who will save us and guide us and be born of the spirit implies not only accepting him but wholeheartedly believing and obeying his commandments.

In other words, renewing the mind means beginning to see the world (the way to perceive reality) with God's eyes, and behave according to His will, that is to say, according to his commandments.

So under no circumstances should we ignore that it is the spirit that guides our first decisions according to God's will. and so, we can clearly understand that the spirit-influenced mind always "advises" you to act and behave MORALLY.

Item 6

What is faith

Talking about faith always unleashes passionate controversy over its complexity.

Faith according to the dictionary means:

- Strongly believe or have a lot of confidence in someone or something

- Set of **beliefs** of someone, a group or a multitude of people.

- Confidence, a good concept you have of someone or something... and…

Believe means:

- Consider or accept a thing as true without irrefutable proof of it, for example, "he believes everything they tell him".

- To think or assume that a person or thing is in a certain way, for example, "I believe this is the one right way"; "I didn't think she was so nice"

• Consider or judge a person in a certain way; "I think he's very smart."

• Give you credit, have confidence in what someone says or does.

Therefore, the words "faith" and "believe" are synonymous

From a religious point of view, **faith** means:

In Hebrew:
The word for translating Faith into Hebrew is "Emunah", which means "truth, fidelity, faith, firmness".

This word comes from the same root as the word "Amen". that's why by saying Amen, we are confirming the truth that has been said.

In Greek:
The meaning of the word Faith is "Pistis", which is much simpler and translates as "Trust".

Now, in the Bible, you can see that the word faith has great meaning because it implicitly carries the teaching of a profound message that I will explain in this chapter to understand the resources that science uses without understanding its spiritual connection.

DEPRESSION **doomed**

The bible in different verses tells us what it is faith, how it is achieved, and what its power is:

(Gal 5:22)
Faith is a work of the spirit of God

(Romans 10: 17
 So faith is by hearing, and hearing, by the word of God.

(Mark 10:15)
Indeed, I say unto you, he that does not receive the kingdom of God as a child, shall not enter into it.

(Romans 3: 22)
"... Justice of God through faith in Jesus Christ, for all who believe in him ... "

(2 Tim 3:15)
Since childhood, you have known the Holy Scriptures, which can give you the wisdom that leads to salvation through faith in Christ Jesus.

(Efe 2: 8-9) 8)
"... By grace you are saved by faith; and this is not from you, for it is the gift of God" 9) not by works, so that no one may glorify.

(James 2: 17)
Thus faith, if it has no works, is dead in itself.

(1 Timothy 4:6)
By pointing these things out to your brethren, you will be a good minister of Christ Jesus, nourished by the words of faith and the good doctrine you have followed.

(Gal 1:23)
He who once persecuted us now preaches the faith he once wanted to destroy.

(Jude 1:3)
"... exhorting them to fight ardently for the faith that was once and for all given to the Saints.

(Romans 1: 12)
... that is, to be mutually comforted by the faith that is common to you and me.

(Luke 7:50)
But he said unto the woman, Your faith has saved thee, go in peace.

(Luke 18:42)
Jesus said to him: receive your sight, your faith has saved you

(2 Corinthians 5: 7)
(because by faith we walk, not by sight)

(1 Thessalonians 5: 8)
"... with the armor of faith and love, and with the hope of salvation as an elm. "

(1 Peter 5:9)
"... resist firm in the faith,... "

(1 John 5: 4)
For all that is born of God overcomes the world, and this is the victory that has overcome the world, our faith.

(1 Peter 1:9)
gaining the end of your faith, which is the salvation of your souls. Notwithstanding all of the above quotations, there is also **"false faith"** and it is more common than one can imagine.

(Hebrews 11:6)
But without faith it is impossible to please God; because it is necessary that the one who approaches God believe that there is him and that he is an award-winner of those who seek Him.

(John 2: 23-25) 23)
When Jesus was in Jerusalem during the Passover feast, many believed in His name by seeing the signs He was making. 24) But Jesus, on the other hand, did not trust them, because he knew them all, 25) and he did not need anyone to bear witness to man, because he knew what was inside man.

(Romans 10:14)
How, then, will they invoke the one they have not believed in? And how will they believe in the one you haven't heard of? And how will they hear without being preached?

James 2: 19)
Of course, you think God is one. You're good; also demons believe and tremble.

I do not believe in the fulfillment of miracles "a la carte" even if they are asked with great faith, to me, miracles happen not at someone's request but by the very nature and wisdom of God. God will only know how, when and to whom... we can only hope that it will.

We do not need a letter of recommendation for God to grant us the grace of forgiveness or any other gift he gives to any of his children, without distinction.

Besides, I hope that you will agree with me that just because a person does not believe in such miracles, it does not mean that God would punish or avenge, or that he would not be given a miracle if I needed it. God gives us what we need at the right time, to believers or not because we are all part of His creation and he knows our strengths and weaknesses.

Not everyone who approaches God has faith, many do so as a last resort after they could not be happy through money, pleasure, or power

Item 7

What is suffering

Many people know the suffering, some since we were born and others are just beginning.

Each person can understand suffering differently but we must and are able to realize that something is happening to us that we do not like or that does not make us feel good and that at the same time makes us see ourselves as "abnormal" people (sick and going with pain)

There are many books that speak of the suffering caused by physical pain which origin can come from a mental illness, and depending on each person, symptoms can vary however there may be many coincidences, for example:

- Not feeling well about what you have or what you are
- Not accepting the reality around us
- Feeling rejected
- Feeling sick
- Thinking you're not capable of many things

We must be able to recognize that these kinds of symptoms are something "abnormal" and accept that we do not know what to do but that we want to be healthy, that is, to return to "normality".

We would like things to be different, we would like to be convinced that we have everything and that we lack nothing, as well as to know that we are as capable as others

When we realize that we are suffering, we sought help at those for whom we were "educated" taught to do it, that is our family, friends, and others close to us.

In Western culture and mainly in Latin America, much of education is based on customs and traditions, leaving scientific and technological advances as secondary.

When someone feels bad or says that they are doing badly, one of the first counsel they receive is to "pray" to God, to the "Virgin Mary" or to the "Virgin of Guadalupe" or to one of the saints who are venerated with great devotion.

And believe it or not, when you do it with a strong conviction this works because by doing so, you are freeing yourself from the responsibility of taking charge of yourself and without you noticing it... you relax, you destress and that favors the better functioning of your body and mind.

This custom is usually strengthened when after the "sick" has tried the most socially accepted remedies, i.e. visiting the doctor, the healer or even some charlatans that offer supernatural cures.

Only in this way, and after exhausting the most common practices without gotten what was desired, is when one seeks the "spiritual" side, that is when you think of God.

Many people, seeking God's help, approach the churches and some of them, and there, in addition to praying and asking for the suffering, certain "ministries" are carried out that seeks to help a more prompt and effective recovery; and in fact, that is why churches or institutions such as the Scientology or the Scientific Christ (among many others) have emerged as some others that rely on astrology, metaphysics or quantum physics practice their own methods to help the person suffering to achieve its optimal state physically and emotionally.

All churches, even the most conservative and even if many of them do not recognize it or do not realize it, use a methodology based mainly on scientific rather than spiritual or faith aspects.

As I discussed in my book "A New God," before seeking help in church to be "normal" or regain the health and harmony of body and mind, I also sought solutions through psychological therapy and agreed to take medications that would help me solve my fundamental problem, that is, clinical depression until I learned that in churches and some other institutions could help me and so look, I found and participated in countless ministries ("courses" or "religious" events) that offered the help that I wanted to find... without imagining in those moments that what I would suddenly find was "A New God".

By way of summary, I want to say that throughout of this whole search process that formally began more or less in 2004, and that for me ended at the end of 2018, when I sadly realized that every attempt to feel "normal" had been failed , I decided to stop looking for new options, because I know there may be more than I could seriously try for the rest of my life... Besides, with the options I knew and with all the information I collected, I was sure that I had the necessary and sufficient elements to create my own method... and so it came up: "Targeted Introspection."

However, I will always be open to other work aimed at the same thing, but I will no longer spend time "experimenting" with "unproven techniques" or "experimental methods" that do not present a clear and objective proposal, i.e. I will no longer accept without having asked and understood how it works so that I can consciously participate and not feel just a guinea pig.

What was supposed to have worked better was the antidepressant medication treatment prescribed by doctors who should presumably be sure of their effectiveness, although of course, they are not the creators of the drugs and only they prescribe from what their representatives from the big pharmaceutical laboratories tell them, they believe it but never verify it, they do not have the technical and scientific resources to do so and only leave a mark on the results when they document their ineffectiveness in the medical records of their patients.

Different cultures and religious groups other than Christianity may or may not have the same perception about the origin of the human being.

But for those of us born under the influence of Judeo-Christianism and not only by FAITH but by reason, too, we have understood and accepted that the Bible is the word of God that speaks to us of his will; we know that God is omniscient, omnipotent, and omnipresent and that therefore everything he created is perfect, including us human beings who are in His image and likeness.

Still, it must be remembered that Satan (a Hebrew word of origin meaning the enemy, the adversary, the one who opposes divinity) is "the God of this world" (2 Cor 4:4), and has been present since the beginning of time trying to prevent the will of God our creator.

Gen 2: 16-17 "And God commanded man, saying, from every tree in the garden thou shalt eat" "But from the tree of science of good and evil thou shalt not eat; because the day you eat from it, you will certainly die.

Gen 3: 1 "But the snake was more cunning... It told the woman, how has God said not to eat from every tree in the orchard?"

The serpent is Satan deceiving the woman into disobeying God's will. She thought she knew, but she didn't realize that the devil already has almost 5 thousand years of experience in cheating.

This is how human beings began to be "abnormal" when temptation and disobedience found complicity with pleasure; and when the disobedient realized what they had done, they immediately began to pay the consequences. They began to repent and feel ashamed that they had discovered the nudes of each other, as well as fearing the punishment God might impose on them. **They began to suffer.**

That was only the beginning of many calamities and tragedies that would be unleashed in life for all humans for not abiding by God's will.

We have all always accused each other and point out our faults and flaws, self-deceiving us or sometimes being sincerely convinced, even if that sincere conviction does not correspond to the truth, for we have all learned "the truth" in a way very personal and according to the environment around us.

DEPRESSION **doomed**

And then we hurt ourselves by not being able to help us but on the contrary, betraying us, abusing our social position pretending to be more or better than others. therefore suffering will not cease to exist until the kingdom of God comes to us, that is until we are able to "renew our minds" by another that allows us to fulfill God's will.

In the meantime, through the method, I have developed (Targeted Introspection) each of us can do something to improve our lives and find our best version to live in harmony with the universe.

Item 8

What is "mental illness"

"The Mayo Clinic says mental illness is also known as a mental health disorder and refers to a wide range of health conditions that affect your mood, thinking, and behavior.

Examples of mental illness include depression, anxiety disorders, schizophrenia, eating disorders and addictive behaviors."

Many people have "mental health problems" from time to time. However, a mental health problem becomes a personality disorder when signs and symptoms are ongoing causing stress and affecting your ability to function.

Symptoms of mental illness can vary depending on the disorder, circumstances, and other factors, they can affect emotions, thoughts, and behaviors.

Examples of symptoms include:

- Feelings of sadness or discouragement
- Excessive worries or fears
- Intense feelings of guilt or resentment
- Confused thoughts or reduced ability to concentrate

- Ups and downs and radical mood changes
- Away from friendships and activities
- Significant tiredness, low energy, and sleep problems
- Disconnection from reality (delirium), paranoia or hallucinations
- Inability to cope with the problems or stresses of daily life
- Drug or alcohol abuse
- Major changes in eating habits
- Changes in sexual desire (inappropriateness, impotence, weariness)
- Excess anger, hostility or violence (unexpected reactions)
- Suicidal thinking or wanting to be dead

Thus, it is possible that almost everyone can find reflection with any of these symptoms, however, we must not lose sight that we ourselves are who must know if what we are living is eventual or constant.

A "mental illness" can make you feel miserable and cause problems in your daily life, at school, at work, or in interpersonal relationships.

In most cases, symptoms can be controlled with a combination of medications, talk therapy (psychotherapy) and most importantly FE.

After all the paths I walked during my search for God, I realized that the human being had been created to function perfectly, that is, in a "normal" way; and to understand why some people don't, it is necessary to know the origin and the environment in which each individual grew up.

Relying on Judeo-Christian theology, which teaches us that all God's creation was perfect including the human being, this is where we must begin to understand what it is to "be well" and what it is to "be wrong", so that we can differentiate between "normal" and "abnormal", this last term is the one that encloses bad function or diseases related to human beings and other aspects of life.

God created the universe perfectly and there is no reason to doubt it, for as I explain in my book "A New God"... When an artist makes a creation, he does so in order to be admired and accepted and for the purpose of transcending and staying, and not to destroy it or to face the frustration of imperfect work.

And even if all this is "subjective" by its theological foundations, is there a better way to explain our essence, could we believe that God was wrong, or that intentionally he created os unequal to provoke envy and suffering?

I don't think so, but you have the right, privilege, and opportunity to live with your own convictions, and if those serve you and have helped you transcend... why not share them?

DEPRESSION **doomed**

It is millions of human beings who are seeking understanding and relief from our suffering and that we are hopeful that one day something or someone will make it so.

Surely the human being was born in equal conditions but, of course, there has always been the need or convenience for an individual or a group of individuals to make decisions and guide others, and in that process, there has never been a lack of who feels badly treated and rebelled.

When unequal treatment happens, there is group division and competition begins for a better "slice" of life.

This division and that competition become exponential and so, there is no choice but to recognize that all of us who are alive today come from one of these groups.

This book is not intended to explain how many groups could be generated, with different ideas, longings, and values in the great world society, but yes, we can say that the result of this gigantic process has produced individuals:

"NORMAL"	"ABNORMAL"
Proud	Unhappy
Rich	Poor
Smart	Ignorant
Workers	Idle
Compassionate	Cruel

Charitable	Spiteful
Grateful	Ungrateful
Healthy	Sick
Creative	Destructive
Prudent	Overtime
Loyal	Treacherous

Etcétera.

When "abnormals" realize they are, they often try and pretend to be "normal," but find multiple impediments that cause feelings of helplessness, frustration, and inferiority, as well as a clear conviction that they could hardly become as they wished.

However, within the global society we all interact and so we mix "normal" with "abnormals" but "appearances" deceive and many pretend to impersonate someone better who we really are and that's how we aspire to climb the ladder, hoping to find in that sea of confusion someone to help us, but in that attempt we become let down and get frustrated and life loses meaning and then an inner rebellion begins against oneself or... against God.

As a result of this frustration we become "sick", we become vengeful, spiteful, envious, etc., and that does not help us get where we want and that makes us apathetic and antisocial and our being is filled with bitterness, pain, and hopelessness.

DEPRESSION **doomed**

That is why when at some point we feel accepted and see that we are welcomed, for a moment we forget the "illness", there is a great change, we feel happy and we forget that we have been rejected by others, we get a new emotion that motivates us to move on... we should all hug and smile.

That would be medicine for all... but as we all deceive ourselves, we become disbelieving and we continue to feel let down and betrayed and become unsafe and unproductive and when everything we tried to live better didn't work, it's when we remember that maybe God could help us.

Everything negative that happens in the process of wanting to be "normal" leads us to manifest our discomfort in different ways, whether lying, hurting, stealing, betraying, abusing others, or simply avoiding reality, wanting to live our pain in silence without others noticing.

This is what in society is reflected as "mental illness" and depending on different variants is known as "anxiety", "depression", "bipolarity", "psychosis", "schizophrenia", etc.

This is nothing more than the manifestation of the lack of interest or motivation to continue competing in an unequal struggle and the fear of being increasingly excluded or rejected by society.

Other facts published by NAMI,

October 2019:
Six myths and facts about mental illness
By Sky Lea Ross October 01, 2019

The stigma associated with mental illness is now called "sanity." Like racism or sexism, it is a form of oppression and discrimination. And there is a lot of sanity and misinformation around the mental illnesses still present in our society.

It's up to us, the mental health community, to educate others and make things clear.

Here are some of the common misconceptions people do and what they need to know.

Myth1: If you have a mental illness you're "crazy."
Fact: It's simple and plain, having a mental illness doesn't mean you're "crazy." It means you're vulnerable. It means you have a disease with challenging symptoms, the same as someone with a disease like diabetes. While mental illness can alter your thinking, destabilize your moods or separate your perception of reality, that doesn't mean you're "crazy." It means you're human and susceptible to disease, just like anyone else.

Myth2: People with mental illness are violent and dangerous.

Fact: In recent years, the United States has had an increase in mass violence.

Every time these tragedies take place, the media rushes to judge the suspects and label them "mentally disturbed" or "mentally ill." In reality, hate is not a mental illness. Only 5% of violent crimes in the United States are committed by people with severe mental illness.

The unfortunate truth is that people with mental illness are more likely to be victims of violence than perpetrators. There is no reason to fear a person with a mental illness just for his diagnosis.

Myth 3: People with bipolar disorder are moody.
Fact: Bipolar disorder does not cause mood swings. Causes cycles that last weeks or months. People often throw around the term "bipolar" to describe the weather. When they say this, it gives in to the severity of the condition and creates misinformation about what bipolar disorder really is.

Bipolar disorder causes you to have episodes in which you experience mania (high energy, rampant thoughts, inability to sleep, great ideas or perspectives, etc.) and depressive states (feeling very slow, sad, suicidal, having low self-esteem, inability to concentrate, etc.) These extreme highs and lows take turns, but they do not change or sway from one moment to the next.

Myth 4: Post-traumatic stress disorder (PTSD) is only a military man's disease.
Fact: Stress disorder is post-mortem ly, not just a military disease. Anyone can have PTSD.

A victim of rape or sexual assault, a victim of domestic abuse, a survivor of a natural disaster, someone who has suffered a loss or even a person who did not face any violence or physical threats directly, but who went on to witness another person who did it (i.e. vicar vicar himself (i.e. trauma).

 Symptoms include having flashbacks of that event or events, nightmares/night terrors, anxiety/panic attacks, taking precautions to avoid reminders or "triggers" of the event, reacting in a way as if the event is re-occurring Etc.

Myth 5: Psychiatric medications are bad.
Fact: People tend to believe that psychiatric medicine is harmful. That, or believe that psychiatric medications are simply "happy pills" and "an easy way out" for those with mental illness to avoid dealing with their problems. Again, this is simply not true.

Like any other harmful medical condition, mental illness remains a disease. For many with mental illness, medication is necessary, just as it would be for a diabetic taking insulin. For some people with mental illness, medications are needed to survive.

For others, such as those with mild to moderate depression, anxiety, or ADHD, medications can help relieve symptoms so they can function normally. And having regular therapy combined with medications can greatly improve quality of life.

Myth 6: Seeking help for mental illness will lead to overeating and worsening symptoms.

Fact: I know it's hard to reach someone about having a mental illness, especially since they are so commonly misunderstood and people who aren't familiar with the mental illness tend to think that people are the way they are because of nature, personality or attitude. But when you have the strength, courage, and courage to open up to someone else, you're working to alleviate the stigma, increase awareness, empower yourself, grow as a person, and promote understanding of mental health. So don't let perceptions of others scare you from getting the help you need.

It is important that we prevent social constructions from framed people as violent or "crazy" because they have a disease that is beyond their control.

People with mental illnesses can work
By Katherine Ponte, BA, JD, MBA, NYCPS-P, CPRP October 21, 2019

I was unemployed for many years while I was sicker. During that time, I felt useless and dependent.

Why? Due to:

- The debilitating impacts of mental illness.
- The fear of having to explain my stained resume due to multiple hospitalizations and depressive episodes.
- The awareness that nothing I'd done before I got sick seemed to tell.
- The prospect of having to start over.
- The stigma that told me I couldn't work.

Stigma tells people with mental illness that we are not ambitious, motivated, intelligent or capable. He says we are unable to manage stress, too sick and even potentially dangerous.

However, these are all myths, and the common belief that people with the disease cannot work is a myth.

Unfortunately, these misconceptions combined with a lack of support prevent many people with mental illness from working.

According to data from the 2010 survey, "employment rates declined with the increased severity of mental illness." And "People with severe mental illness are less likely than people with mental illness, mild or moderate to be employed after age 49."

DEPRESSION **doomed**

This is a problem that needs our attention. People with mental illnesses can, should and often need to work.

The social costs of unemployment and underemployment for people living with mental illnesses are incalculable: deteriorating health, additional health care costs, a financial struggle for families, among many others.

 In addition, work gives a source of purpose and allows us to contribute to our families and society.

Sustained employment is an incredibly important factor for recovery. And most people with mental illness can succeed with the right support.

Item 9

Consequences of disease

It is very likely that medical science will not be able to diagnose all diseases and if it finds a "new unknown disease" it usually labels it as "syndrome..." to emphasize that this disease resembles another one they know but that it has certain characteristics that make it different and add the surname of the one who noticed it.

Likewise, science has been tasked with investigating what can cause disease, and over time they have discovered that many diseases are generated by microscopic organisms such as bacteria or viruses.

These microscopic organisms are living organisms and have found in the human and animal bodies an ideal environment to survive through cells and tissues that can constitute one of our internal organs.

The virus needs a cell to live, the bacteria instead are in the environment. Some bacteria live in our bodies and do not cause us problems, they are found in water and in the ground, on the surfaces of the food we eat and on the surfaces we touch.

It is easy to understand that when these micro-organisms invade the human body if they are not fought in a timely manner they can wreak havoc that can lead to death.

Symptoms that may occur in a person by microscopic invasion usually manifest in a very noticeable way, such as vomiting, bleeding, welts, blindness, deafness, partial or total paralysis of the body, etc.

However, it would be very difficult to try to attribute any of these symptoms to a mental health problem, although some have claimed that due to stress the immune system can become so weak, to the extent that the body runs out of defenses to protect.

However, we also know and it has been scientifically proven that stress can trigger a number of health problems in the human body, for example, exhaustion, sexual disorders, constipation, skin infections, acne, memory loss, overweight and obesity, hair loss, back pain, insomnia, etcetera.

On Wikipedia I found the following article:
"Stress (from Latin stringere "squeeze" through its derivative in English stress "material fatigue") is a physiological reaction of the organism in which

various defense mechanisms come into play to deal with a situation that is perceived as threatening or increased demand.

Physiological or biological is an organism's response to a stress factor such as an environmental condition or a stimulus.

Stress is a body's way of reacting to a challenge.

According to the stressful event, the body's way of responding to stress is through the sympathetic nervous system of activation that results in the fight-or-flight response.

Because the body cannot maintain this state for long periods of time, the parasympathetic system tends to return the body to more normal physiological conditions (homeostasis).

In humans, stress usually describes a negative condition (distrés) or conversely a positive condition (eustrés), which can have a mental, physical and even welfare or discomfort effect in a human being, or even in another species of animal."

Then, it should be emphasized that stress can be the trigger for various disorders or diseases that can range from anxiety, distress, depression, bipolarity, to any other type of physical disease... and if the laws (legal, social, moral) are also broken, it is very likely that an emotional imbalance will unlash and can become the psychosomatic cause of any of the different manifestations shown below:

Physical
Stress, tiredness, weakness, fragility, sweating, insomnia, digestive problems, diabetes, tachycardia, high or low blood pressure, sexual impotence, frigidity, heart attack, embolism, cancer, etc. underlying that all these problems can also result from psychosomatic causes.

Mental or emotional:
Feelings of superiority or inferiority, insecurity, jealousy, fear, shame, lack of motivation, nervousness, distrust, sadness, anxiety, anguish, despair, envy, spite, guilt, desires to die, etc.

Social:
- Inability to cope with the stress or problems of daily life
- Loss of job or difficulty in maintaining or obtaining it
- Problems with husband, children, parents, siblings, etc.
- Distancing from friendships.
- Not considered for social events.
- Conflicting, generates fear and mistrust
- Drug and alcohol intolerance and abuse

- Etc.

Non-compliance with legal laws leads to the payment of fines, deprivation of liberty and often too capital punishment, i.e. death.

Non-compliance with social laws leads to segregation or expulsion from the community.
Non-compliance with moral laws leads to feelings of guilt, sadness, and desolation.

And failure to comply with any of these 3 laws may arise a punishment that can become insufferable... "emotional imbalance" or "loss of sanity."

This happens because no one resists the consequence of being "expelled from paradise", that is, we all want to live in freedom, we all want to be accepted into our society and live with dignity and, that is how it should be if we follow the standards of normalcy.

Many of the factors that affect the emotional imbalance are external and we have no control over them as we are only victims of circumstances, but the imbalance by the violation of laws, we can only adjudicate directly to ourselves, and in either case, the consequences can manifest as physical, mental or combined illness.

It is difficult to establish what motivates us to violate the laws but somehow we can mention as root causes: injustice, poverty, betrayal, corruption, extortion, heartbreak, etc. which lets us see that one fault leads to another and another and another.

This is how everything becomes abnormal and in each individual, it can manifest itself in different ways because it depends on who, when, how or why it has been affected since, in addition, it is not the same if it happens in early childhood, adolescence, adulthood or old age.

The human being was designed and created by God to live and "work" well, but as it has already been explained, "the evil one" always stands in the way to prevent it happen.

This is a reality that no one can escape from the moment we are born because we are born to parents who have surely committed faults and who have or still are paying the consequences.

So as we grow, our parents and closest family members could prevent us from the consequences of breaking the law, only if they have learned the standards of normality under "the law."

Therefore, it is necessary that in order to avoid a misunderstanding of the laws, we realize and commit to accept that we have to renew our minds, which involves clarifying and updating our information about what we have learned so far and accepted as good.

Item 10

Medical aspects

For more than a century, doctors of those times called disorders or mental illness different manifestations of personality not common... Sigmund Freud found that many of these "disorders" were due to repressed feelings or emotions, and many of those emotions were related to aspects of sexuality.

Repressed sexuality can definitely be one of the causes that lead to personality disorders, and I think by its times (the early 1900s) this must have been a very common cause because of the fear that was mainly in women of practicing acts related to sexuality outside of marriage.

Although it seems to me that the most important thing is to emphasize that any kind of repressed feelings or emotions or the denial of them such as frustration, inferiority, fear, sadness, fury, etc., can trigger all kinds of "abnormal" behaviors "

Other scientists thought the problem was in the brain and in their eagerness to check it out, they came to practice monstrous acts such as lobotomy and uncontrolled electric shocks.

DEPRESSION **doomed**

Note that over time many have pretended to know the origin of what has been known as mental illness, but to this day, it seems that we are still in obscurantism.

Undoubtedly great advances have been made in the knowledge of certain functions performed by the brain but I think that there is still a long way to go to understand the intricate functioning of the networks involved in the personality of the individual... We talk about the interaction of trillions of neurons and chemical processes that take place at every moment.

It seems like sci-fi the fact that back in some lab they are developing a "magic" pill that will solve the problems of your life... and I say it this way because, until today, no one knows how the chemical imbalance originates in the production of hormones in the brain, and so far it is known that "scientists" have only found how to help the brain continue to produce the hormones in the amounts proper, without that solving the cause... as it is happening with helping the pancreas in the production of insulin.

But I insist, to be known today, they have not discovered that or how this chemical imbalance originates, which is why their medications cannot "cure" depression, bipolarity or any other similar problem.

Many have reported that this "disease" may be of genetic origin, and probably is, but they are also not sure or have found the cause why a chromosome in the "DNA" chain alters its function.

Dr. Boris Cirulnik (Psychologist and Psychiatrist), Professor at the University of Tolon, France, author of 36 books, including "Psychotherapy of God", states that the probability that a disease has genetic origin does not exceed even 5%.

Others, including the aforementioned Dr. Cirulnik, have said that the origin of the problem is psychological, and I could lean more towards thinking that this may be the real reason for the disease, for it is true that external stimuli generate thoughts, and thoughts emotions that the brain detects and interprets at any event, and if this event is negative the brain can issue instructions that alter the proper functioning of the glands responsible for the production of hormones or any other chemical element. However, it should not be lost sight that usually these external stimuli are produced by the sociocultural environment of the individual, which can turn a social problem into a health problem.

Laura Llorens,

(https://psicologiaymente.com/psicologia/bloqueo-mental)

Social Worker, Diploma in Social Work and with a postgraduate degree in Forensic Sciences for Social

DEPRESSION **doomed**

Workers. She currently works in a science museum. She is passionate about the brain on a biological and psychological level; developed the following article:

In the words of psychiatrist Manuel Escudero, the mental blockade is defined as: "interruption of a brain process that does not allow us to start or terminate any activity or situation.

This phenomenon can be seen as the impossibility of following a line of thought that affects our behaviors, undermines our effectiveness and limits our potential to achieve our ultimate goal."

The mental blockage is neither good nor bad. In the world of psychology, we do not talk about black and white, you have to move more by the nuances.

In the case of mental blockages, if we stick to the definition, we are talking about a defense mechanism which objective is to protect ourselves from a situation that overcomes us. So its something that protects us, is good for us and exists for a reason...

But like so many things, the good in excess can be dangerous, and these mechanisms are no exception.

The problem comes when they are used excessively or at times when not only are they not necessary, but they make it difficult for us to get out of a relatively easy situation that we inadvertently lengthen.

The blockage has a multi-causal origin: traumatic experiences, lack of self-esteem, anxiety, depression, lack of confidence or knowledge... All this leads to a lack of response to a situation, which in turn leads to more anxiety, frustration, and stress.

At the brain level, a University of Canada conducted a study showing how hormones released in stress affect the brain regions related to memory and spatial orientation and influence the imbalance of Neurotransmitters. This fact, at the same time, influences the moments when we feel we are blank and we cannot remember meaningful ideas or goals to pursue.

At the same time, the fact of noticing us vulnerable and not knowing what to do leads us to feel more anxious, which in turn fuels the mental blockage, etc. An indecision loop is created that sometimes costs a break.

DEPRESSION **doomed**

Item 11

Statistics

The World Health Organization "WHO" says:

It is estimated that approximately 20% of the world's children and adolescents have mental disorders or problems and that about half of the mental disorders develop before the age of 14.

Similar types of disorders are observed in all cultures. Neuropsychiatric disorders are among the leading causes of disability among young people.

However, the regions of the world with the highest population percentages under the age of 19 have the least mental health resources. Most low- and middle-income countries have only one child psychiatrist for every million to four million people.

More than 800,000 people commit suicide each year, and suicide is the second leading cause of death in the 15-29 age group. There are indications that for every adult who commits suicide there are more than 20 who try. 75% of suicides occur in low- and middle-income countries.

Mental disorders and harmful alcohol use contribute to many suicides.

Early identification and effective treatment are critical to ensuring that these people get the care they need.

The ignorance and stigmatization surrounding mental illness are widespread. Despite effective treatments, there is a belief that it is not possible to treat mental disorders, or that people with them are difficult, unintelligent, or incapable of making decisions.

Such stigmatization can lead to ill-treatment, rejection, and isolation, and deprive people of affected medical care and support. Within the health system, it is very common for these people to receive treatment in institutions that are more like human warehouses than places to heal.

National Alliance on Mental Illness (NAMI)

Prevalence of mental illness:

- Approximately 1 in 5 adults in the United States (46.6 million) experience mental illness in a given year.

- Approximately 1 in 25 adults in the United States (11.2 million) experience severe mental illness in a given year that substantially interferes with or limits one or more important life activities.

- Approximately 1 in 5 13-18-year-olds (21.4%) experienced a serious mental disorder at some point in their life.

- For children ages 8 to 15, the estimate is 13%.

- 1.1% of adults in the United States live with schizophrenia.

- 2.6% of adults in the United States live with bipolar disorder.

- 6.9% of adults in the United States—16 million—had at least one major depressive episode in the past year.

- 18.1% of adults in the United States experienced an anxiety disorder such as post-traumatic stress disorder, obsessive-compulsive disorder, and specific phobias.

- Among the 20.2 million adults in the United States who experienced substance use disorder, 50.5%—10.2 million adults—had a co-occurring mental illness.

<u>Social Status:</u>

- It is estimated that 26% of homeless adults who remain in shelters live with serious mental illness and an estimated 46% live with serious mental illness and/or substance use disorders

- Approximately 20% of state prisoners and 21% of local prisoners have "a recent history" of a mental health condition.

- 70% of young people in juvenile justice systems have at least one mental health condition and at least 20% live with severe mental illness.

- Only 41% of adults in the United States with a mental health condition received mental health services in the past year. Among adults with severe mental illness, 62.9% received mental health services last year.

- Just over half (50.6%) children with a mental health condition of 8 to 15 years who received mental health services in the previous year.

- African Americans and Hispanic Americans each use mental health services at about half the rate of Caucasian Americans and Asian Americans at about one-third of the rate.

- Half of all chronic mental illnesses begin at age 14; three-quarters at 24. Despite effective treatment, there are long delays (sometimes decades) between the first onset of symptoms and when people receive help.

Consequences of lack of treatment:

- Severe mental illness costs the United States $193.2 billion in lost profits per year.

- Mood disorders, such as major depression, distal disorder, and bipolar disorder, are the third most common cause of hospitalization in the United States for both young people and adults ages 18 to 44.

- People living with severe mental illnesses face an increased risk of chronic diseases. Adults in the United States living with a serious mental illness die on average 25 years earlier than others, largely due to treatable medical conditions.

- More than a third (37%) of students with a mental health condition of 14 to 21 years and older who are cared for by neglecting special education, the highest dropout rate of any disability group.

- Suicide is the tenth leading cause of death in the United States and the second leading cause of death for people aged 10 to 34.

- More than 90% of people who die by suicide show symptoms of a mental health condition.

- Between 18 and 22 veterans die by suicide every day.

Item 12

The principle of change

To start a change, we need to know who we are and who we want to become, and then have a plan to achieve it.

For the purposes of this job, knowing who we are means being aware that something is wrong with us, and knowing who we want to become means having a desire to be well, to be "normal."

As has already been mentioned, to understand who we want to become, we need to know the standards against which we can measure ourselves and for that purpose, we will base the Bible whose word we accept as the Law and the will of God.

Why the Bible?, Regardless of whether the Bible:

- Has been written by 40 or more people
- Inspired by God
- Is or not a historical book
- Present contradictions
- Is sometimes incongruous
- Contain violence
- Talk about Sacrifices
- Tell Romances
- Share Poetry
- Etcétera.

The Bible is full of wisdom and you can be sure that it was not written by teenage boys smoking marihuana but by the older men who witnessed the perverted conduct of their fellow men describing the consequences that proved disastrous and knowing that if they continue like this, they could end up extinguishing humanity.

The Bible was written to reflect an all-time photograph, it was written to leave the message for posterity so that the human being reflects and is able to amend their mistakes.

Later, in the topic of "Ethical and Moral Principles" you will see what was written and I am sure you will understand that if God had written it in person, he would have written it as it is, for it is nothing more than the desire to preserve his creation, protect ourselves and make us know how we should behave... so that we can live in his kingdom.

Although as I have also mentioned, for me, there is more than one sacred book that could guide our course according to God's will regardless of the name by which others call it.

Therefore, we will immediately begin by seeing what are the foundations of God's "law."

Item 12.1

Theology

Surely we at some point in our lives have questioned where we came from, how we came from, and what our purpose is.

And these questions have been answered through the Bible and other "sacred" or scientific books; the answers that have been given, for many, have been indisputable, but for many others, they have been questionable.

Now, we all have the right to raise our voice and express our agreement or disagreement and in this case it would be highly recommended that before rejecting what the Bible teaches us, you wonder if you know or might have a better option to offer for the whole world can live in harmony and if you would also be committed to spreading your foundations to make them available to anyone who needs it.

The Bible talks us about the creation of the entire universe and teaches us that God created us in his image and likeness and whether we like it or not, there is no way to disprove it, for although there are multiple versions... none has been universally validated and accepted. Moreover, if we do not understand the concept of the Faith, it will be more difficult for us to understand the divine message.

Then, from the Bible we know that God is perfect as perfect is his creation and as I mentioned in my book "A New God" creation implies art and the purpose of the artist is that his creation is known, remains and transcends in order for someone to see it, understand it, appreciate it and enjoy it.

And if God made us perfect, that means:

1. We are born healthy with body and mind

2. The philosopher John Locke in ancient Rome through his epistemological theory of "tabula rasa" established that at birth the human being comes with the blank mind i.e. it is clean, and I would add; except for the basic information of survival , nodding to the theory of "inanitism" that holds that the mind is born with knowledge

3. We were created as we are, and we are all worth, the same and we are equal

4. We deserve to be loved and respected

5. We have the ability to accomplish anything

6. We have intelligence, imagination, creativity, intuition, and we know how to discern

7. We all can and deserve to live in peace

So if we were created by God like this, then our minds wonder why many of us are not happy, why we suffer, why we get sick, why we are poor? And because of these and many doubts, we rebel, we feel deceived, mocked, and sometimes even resentful of God.

However, we must not forget that although God is and means all that is good, and that if there is light, there is also darkness and that there is also "Satan" who is the prince of this world, the enemy, the adversary, the opposite of God.

That is why the wisdom of the Bible prevents us from the tricks that Satan can use to turn us away from God, that is, the way of good.

This was the case from the beginning of creation when Eve was "tempted" by Satan in the form of a serpent, and let us not lose sight that today before us it (Satan) can take any other form, even that of God that we do not know and have only imagined (John 1 18 "No one has ever seen God: the only Son, who is in the father's mind, he has counted it") and we may not notice it unless we are properly prepared with the knowledge of the word of God.

So this is how we explain why we have all sinned, that is, we have failed to follow God's will. because Eve and Adam were weak and that is what they taught their descendants and since then we all failed, we always fail because curiosity and temptation are part of our nature (Gen 8:21 "... because the attempt of man's heart has been bad since his youth. or, because traces of the human heart are bad from his childhood..."

Words can vary depending on the version of the bible being consulted, but something very important here, is to understand that the heart in principle contains all the goodwill of God and then it might turn into the wrong heart by the influence of the deceiver)

This is why we human beings have made all kinds of mistakes in our lives and those mistakes have had consequences that make us feel guilty or resentful and from there the shame, revenge, and hatred that has brought us nothing but displeasure suffering.

And yet God gives us the opportunity to "return to his path" by reborn and renewing our minds. trusting that only in HE we can trust and find peace, and we can do that through our discernment, for as we grow, we have learned to distinguish between "good" and "evil"... but for some reason and without realizing it many times we choose "evil" by pretending that we have made the decisions that best suited, forgetting that it is not us who must decide what is good or bad but only the will of God that is already written.

DEPRESSION **doomed**

I would very much like it to be understood that not all of our bad choices should be awarded directly to ourselves since we are only a replica of our ancestors, that is, each of us has learned the concepts of good and evil according to what our parents and close people have taught us and every time we have to make a decision we do it only with the only information we have, and at that very moment where we could have made a decision impulsively, we can't figure it out if we did well or did wrong because at the end of the day our trust departed with what was taught to us by those who would never deceive us or advise us to something that could hurt us… our parents.

We must be aware that in many cases, our ancestors did not have the opportunity for higher education and almost, some of them only learned the basic education of reading and writing, and in other cases not even that. This means that a lot of what they learned was from what they heard and we all know the effect of the "phone game."

Therefore, the time has come to begin to ask ourselves how reliable is the knowledge we have acquired because with that information we analyze, evaluate and perceive life, and what and how things should be and mainly how we perceive ourselves.

This misguided, incorrect or incomplete information ("mental implants") can negatively influence all aspects of our lives, our work, our health, our social relationships with friends and family, as we all have similar basic information and at the same time we all have very own and characteristic information, which often when confronted with others, we fall into disagreements and fights and consequences can come in physical, emotional or social diseases .

Item 12.2

Ethical and moral principles

The word of God—The Law—began to be written from about 1,500 BC to the end of 100 A.D., so today the bible as a whole is 3,500 years old or so.

Throughout this period, the man was writing what God wanted all of us to know.

Among other things, interesting, exciting and moving stories, feats, betrayals, sacrifice, suffering, prophecies, poetry, death, hope, wisdom, repentance, forgiveness and change, etc.

Within these books, we can find what should be considered as the standard of the "normal" and what have been the causes that have led us to "abnormality"... but we can also find out how to start over to get back to the starting point, that is, to "normality"

Human beings have come to question themselves, How should I behave with myself and others? And how should they behave with me?...

More often we believe that we do know how it should be and in the attempt to protect ourselves and seek our safety we say that others do not do the right thing and that is why they make us fail.

If we all behaved as the Bible envisages, we would live in paradise, but it has always been very difficult for all of us to accept the truths of others, so those of us who are Christians by faith or conviction and are willing to live according to God's will, we must know the elements that would help us know what is right and what is wrong, what would be the right attitude or behavior that we should all follow to live in harmony.

Perhaps the last commandment of Jesus would be sufficed:

John 13:34 This new commandment I give you: that you love one another. Just as I have loved you, so must you love one another.

However, even though this commandment might be enough for all of us to live in harmony, it is not so, for the reality is that today each of us seeks to be safe no matter that others can be saved.

Most likely, because many believe that to enjoy the kingdom of God and live an eternal life, it is sufficient to be "saved" by God's grace, and no longer care about continuing to be Christians, or they are in their own way, they have forgotten the true meaning of being a Christian, and they do not realize that by stopping being Christian they continue to incur faults that break harmony and lead to disasters and misfortunes.

Either they ignore or they do not care to properly fulfill God's will, they set aside the fact that faith without works is dead. Paul wrote in 2 Corinthians 5:17, "So if any man is in Christ, he is new creature; old things happened; Behold they are all made new" and James 2: 14-26 says: "And it is that if a brother who is naked or hungry comes to us, and we deny him clothing or food and limit ourselves to offering him good words, then our faith is dead."

Therefore, it is essential to remember what behavior we should all follow to consider ourselves "normal". "Christians", and live in harmony.

The Bible says in 2 Timothy 3: 16 – 17:
16 All Scripture is inspired by God and useful to teach, to rebuke, to correct, to instruct in righteousness, 17 that the man of God may be perfect, equipped for every good work.

So to know the right, you have to know and remember the word of God. "The Law"

Item 12.3

10 Commandments

Exodus 20: 3- 17

I.   3 Have no other gods besides me.

II.   4 Do not make an idol, nor anything that bears resemblance to what is above in heaven…

III.   7 Do not use the name of the Lord… in vain.

IV.   8 Remember the Sabbath, to consecrate it. 9 Work six days, and do in them all that thou shalt do, 10 ...

V.   12 Honor your father and mother...

VI.   13 Do not kill.

VII.   14 Do not commit adultery.

VIII.   15 Do not steal.

IX.   16 Do not give false witness against your neighbor.

X.   17 Do not covet thy neighbor's house: Do not covet his wife, nor his slave, nor his ox, nor his donkey, nor anything that belongs to him.

Item 12.4

7 Deadly sins

The Bible does not classify as such the 7 deadly sins, which in fact were 8 and were called "temptations of the soul" (the 8th was Despair because it meant believing that God was not enough...)

However, there are many authors who have explained this and one of them is Francisco Mario Morales who shared on the Internet (Source: Catholic.net):

"Against these 7 deadly vices or sins, there are 7 virtues that praise the same Scripture"

PRIDE. - (Sir*. 10, 12-18; Prov. 26, 12; Dn. 3, 1 - 6)
* The book Sir-Sirach or Ecclesiastical is part of the Deuteronomic or apocryphal and is located in the Catholic Bible.

It is poorly esteem of himself, which makes him consider himself one higher than others and want to rise above them.

The first sin of pride was committed by the devil when he rebelled against God.

The effects are:

- 1st pride seeks to show the qualities that one believes one has,
- 2nd believes himself capable of everything, and this is the presumption;
- 3rd he wants to appear better than he is and despises his equals or his inferiors.

The virtue opposed to pride is **Humility** (Efe. 4, 2 – 4)

GREED. (Matthew 6, 19 -21; Sir. 31, 1 – 4; Sirac. 13, 20 - 26)
It is an excessive love for material goods and mainly for money.

It is recognized that material goods are overestimated when regardless of illicit means they are willing to acquire, conserve and increase them.

Greed is a great sin; St. Paul calls it idolatry and declares that misers will not enter the Kingdom of Heaven.

Greed makes us the poor, indifferent to the goods of heaven, and even sometimes encourages us to seize the goods of others.

The virtue opposed to Greed is **Goodness** (Gl. 5, 22 – 24)

LUJURIA.- (1 Cor. 6, 9 – 11; Rom. 13, 13; Rom. 1, 18 – 32; Lev. 18. 1 – 23; Gal. 5, 19 - 26)
Addiction, depravity, perversion, deviations and shameful passions.

It is the shameful vice of impurity forbidden by the sixth and ninth commandment.

Lust makes us abhor our religious duties; blind the spirit, harden slowers the heart, harms the health and the most beautiful qualities of the soul.

The ability to love is lost and others are seen as disposable objects (use and discard), and passion is confused as love.

Chastity means the integration of sexuality into the person and, therefore, in the inner unity of man, in his bodily and spiritual being.

It is part of the cardinal virtue of temperance, which tends to imbue passions and appetites of human sensitivity. Among the great sins against chastity are included masturbation, fornication,pornography, and homosexuality.

(Synthesis of the New Catechism 345, 346) The virtue opposed to Lust is **Chastity** (1 Cor. 6, 9) What is chastity? chastity is nothing but the mastery of sexuality for the reason to learn to respect oneself and others

IRA.- (Ecle. 7, 9; Col. 3, 5 – 9; Gn. 4, 8)
Anger is a disorderly movement of the soul that impels us to violently reject what we dislike.

The ordinary causes of anger are the pride and stubborn attachment to one's own ideas.

Anger leads us to blaspheme the Holy Name of God, to avenge one's neighbor, to insult, to hurt, and sometimes to death. Killing is not only taking life, but it is also an attack on dignity and honor.

When God commands us not to kill, He forbids us to harm our own and our neighbor's body or spiritual life.

This sin also violates the 5th. Commandment. Let us see what James tells us about a deadly weapon (Sgo. 3, 1 – 12) The virtue opposed to Anger is **Patience** (2 Tim. 3, 10)

GULA.- (Sir. 37, 29 – 31; Rom. 13, 13)
It's a messy hobby of drinking and eating. Such a hobby is disorderly when you eat or drink with excess or for the only pleasure of satisfying sensuality.

The gluttony is a sin; St. Paul compares those who give themselves to her as idolaters and says that they make her womb a God. The virtue opposed to gluttony is **Moderation** (2 Ped. 1, 5-8)

ENVY. - (Sir. 13, 25 – 26; 14, 9 -19; Gn. 3, 1 – 24)

Envy is a sadness that is felt inside the good of others or a joy guilty of the evil of others.

Envy is a great sin, because:
- 1st directly opposes the love of the neighbor
- 2o makes the one who is a slave to it, like the devil, because, by envy, he now seeks the means of harm.

Envy is a continuous torment and suffering, it gnaws and devours the heart.

Envy begets a great number of sins; unjust suspicion, slander, curses, discord, hatred, and even murder. The virtue opposed to envy is **Charity** (1 Cr. 9, 24 – 27) fraternally that makes taking the worries and joys of others as their own. Love of one's neighbor (1 Cor. 13, 1 – 13).

LAZINESS - (Prov. 6, 9 – 19)
It is an excessive fondness for rest, in negligence, neglect of our duties so as not to impose any effort on us.

There are two kinds of laziness:

- 1st spiritual laziness, which induces us to be apathetic and indifferent to our religious duties;

- 2nd the temporal, which induces us not to recognize and accept the duties of our own state.

DEPRESSION **doomed**

It is the mother of all vices: it mainly engenders idleness and wasted time, the origin of ignorance and incapacity; it produces inconsistency and the futility of life.

The virtue opposed to Laziness is **Diligence** (Prov. 6, 6 – 12) which impels us to fulfill all our duties with accuracy and enthusiasm.

Item 12.5

Other commandments

1 Corinthians 1: 10-11
10 ... that you all agree, and that there are no divisions between you, but that you are entirely united in one feeling and in the same mind. 11...

1 Corinthians 5: 1-2
1 Indeed, it is heard that among you there is immorality, ... to the extent that some have their father's wife. 2 And ye have become arrogant

1 Corinthians 5: 9-11
9 ... that you did not walk in the company of immoral people; 10 I didn't mean ... to the veins and swindlers, or to the idolaters, ... 11 ... I wrote not to walk in the company of ... an immoral, or greedy, or

idolater, or defamer, or drunken person, or con artist; with that one, don't even eat.

1 Corinthians 6: 9-10

9 ... neither the immoral, nor the idolaters, nor the adulterers, nor the effeminate, nor the homosexuals, nor the thieves, nor the beggars, nor the drunks, nor the defamatory, nor the con artists will inherit the kingdom of God.

1 Corinthians 6: 12-13

12 All things are lawful to me, ... 13 ... However, the body is not for fornication, but for the Lord, and the Lord is for the body.

1 Corinthians 6: 18-19

18 Runaway from fornication. All the other sins a man commits are outside the body, but the fornicator sins against his own body. 19 Or know ye not that your body is a temple of the Holy Spirit, that it is in you, which ye have of God, and that ye are not yours?

1 Corinthians 7: 1-5

1 ..., good it is for the man not to touch a woman. 2 ... because of immoralities, that everyone has their own wife, and each has their own husband. 3 That the husband doeth his duty to his wife, and so the woman does it with the husband. 4 A woman has no authority over her own body, but the husband. And also the husband has no authority over his own

body, but the woman. 5 Do not deprive one another, except by common agreement and for a certain time, that Satan may not tempt you because of your lack of self-mastery.

1 Corinthians 10: 13
13... God, who will not allow you to be tempted beyond what you can bear, but with the temptation will also provide the way of escape, so that you may resist it.

1 Corinthians 10: 23-24
23 Everything is lawful, but not all are of benefit. ... 24 No man seeketh his own good, but that of his neighbor.

1 Corinthians 10: 32-33
32 Be not a cause of stumbling to the Jews, nor the Greeks, nor the church of God;   33...

1 Corinthians 11: 29-30
29 For him that eateth and drinks without discerning the body of the Lord correctly, eateth and drinketh judgment unto himself. 30 For this reason, there are many weak and sick among you, and many sleep.

1 Corinthians 13: 29-30
4 Love is patient, it is kind; love is not envious; love is not boastful, it is not arrogant; 5 He does not act unseemly; does not seek his own thing, does not become irritated, does not take into account the evil received; 6 He rejoiceth not of injustice, but rejoiceth with the truth; 7 All suffereth it, believes it all, expects everything, endures everything.

1 Corinthians 13: 11-13
11... when I became a man, I gave things up as a kid. 12... now we see by a mirror, veiledly, ... 13 And now the faith, hope, and love remain, these three; but the greatest of them is love.

1 Corinthians 15: 33-34
33 Let ye not be deceived: Bad companies corrupt good manners. 34 Be sober, as it is appropriate, and stop sinning; because some have no knowledge of God. To your shame, I say so.

2 Corinthians 2: 5-11
5 If any man hath caused sadness,... he's caused it to all of you. 6... 7...   they should forgive him and comfort him so that he is not consumed by excessive sadness. 8... reaffirm your love for him. 9... to see if they pass the test of complete obedience. 10 Whom ye forgive, I forgive him too. In fact, if there was anything to forgive, I have forgiven you out of consideration for you in the presence of Christ, 11 that Satan may not take advantage of us, for we do not ignore his ruse.

2 Corinthians 4: 2-4
2... we have renounced all the shameful thing that is done in secret; we do not act with deception or twist the word of God. On the contrary... 3... 4 The God of this world (Satan) has blinded the minds of these disbelievers, that they may not see the light of the glorious gospel of Christ, which is the image of God.

2 Corinthians 9:6-9

6... He who sows scarcely will scarcely harvest, and he who sows in abundance shall reap abundantly. 7 Each one must give according to what he has decided in his heart, not reluctantly, nor by obligation, for God loves him that giveth with joy. 8 And God can cause all grace to join unto you, ... 9 As is written: "He distributed his goods among the poor; their justice remains forever."

Galatians 5: 14-26

14... the whole law is summed up in one commandment: Love your neighbor as yourself. 15 But if they continue to bite and devour, be careful, let us not end up destroying one another. 16... Live by the Spirit, and you will not follow the desires of sinful nature. 17 For the desired that which is contrary to the Spirit, and the Spirit desired that which is contrary to it. The two oppose each other, so you can't do what you want. 18 But if they are guided by the Spirit, they are not under the law. 19 The works of sinful nature are well known: sexual immorality, impurity, and debauchery; 20 idolatry and witchcraft; hatred, discord, jealousy, outbursts of anger, rivalries, dissensions, 21st selves, and envy; drunkenness, and other similar things. I warn you now, as I did before, that those who practice such things will not inherit the kingdom of God. 22 On the other hand, the fruit of the Spirit is love, joy, peace, patience, kindness, faithfulness, 23 humility, and self-control. There is no law to condemn these things. 24 Those who are of Christ Jesus have crucified sinful nature, with their passions and desires. 25 If the Spirit gives us life, let us be guided by the Spirit. 26 Let us not let vanity lead us to annoy and to envy one another.

Galatians 6: 1-5

1... If someone is caught in a sin, you who are spiritual should restore you with a humble attitude. But take care of each one, because he can also be tempted. 2 Help one another carry their burdens,... 3 If someone believes to be something when in reality it is nothing, he deceives himself. 4 Each one examines his own conduct; and, if you have something to brag about, don't compare yourself to anyone. 5 Let each one bear his own responsibility.

Ephesians 4: 25-32

25... leaving the lie, each one to speak to his neighbor with the truth,... 26 If they are angry, sin not. Do not let anger last you until sunset, 27 or accommodate the devil. 28 He that stole, who stealeth no more, but works honestly. 29 Avoid all obscene conversation... may his words contribute to the necessary building and be a blessing to those who hear 30 Do not aggravate the Holy Spirit of God. 31 Let all bitterness, anger, and anger, cries, and slander, and all form of malice aside. 32 Rather, be kind and compassionate unto one another, and forgive one another, even as God forgave you in Christ.

Ephesians 5: 3-5

3Among you, sexual immorality, nor any kind of impurity or greed, should not be mentioned,... 4 Nor should there be indecent words, foolish conversations or rude jokes,... 5... no one who is greedy (i.e. idolater), immoral or impure will have an inheritance in the kingdom of Christ and of God.

Ephesians 5: 11-14

11 Have nothing to do with the fruitless works of darkness, but rather denounce them, 12 for it is shameless even to mention what the disobedient do in secret. 13 But all that light exposes is made visible, 14 for light is what makes everything visible. That is why it is said: Wake up, you who sleep, rise from the dead, and Christ will enlighten you.

Ephesians 5: 22-24

22 Wives, bear unto your own husbands as to the Lord. 23 For the husband is the head of his wife,... 24 Just as the church submits unto Christ, even wives must submit to their husbands in all things.

Ephesians 5: 28-29

28 Likewise, the husband must love his wife as his own body. He who loves his wife loves himself, 29 for no one has ever hated his own body; on the contrary, it feeds and cares for it, just as Christ does with the church,

Ephesians 6: 1-17

1... obey their parents in the Lord,... 2 Honor thy father and mother ... 3 That you may do well and enjoy a long life on earth. 4 And ye, fathers, do not anger your children but raise them according to the discipline and instruction of the Lord. 5 Slaves, obey their earthly masters with respect and fear, and with the integrity of heart. 6 Do not do it only when they are looking at them, as they who want to earn human favor,... 7 Serve willingly, as one who serves the Lord, and not men, 8... The Lord will reward. for the sake you've done, ... 9 And ye, masters, correspond to this attitude. 10... 11 Put on all the armor of God so that you can face the devil's tricks. 12 For our struggle is not against human beings, but against powers, against authorities, against other powers that dominate this world of darkness, against evil spiritual forces in the heavenly regions. 13... 14 Stand firm, bound with the belt of truth, protected by the armory of righteousness, 15 and footwear with a willingness to proclaim the gospel of peace. 16..., take the shield of faith, with which you can turn off all the kindled arrows of the evil one. 17 Take the helmet of salvation, and the sword of the Spirit, which is the word of God.

Colossians 3: 5-10
5... they make all that is proper to earthly nature die: sexual immorality, impurity, low passions, bad desires, and greed, which is idolatry. 6.... 7 You practiced them at another time when you lived in them. 8 But now also forsake all this: anger, anger, malice, slander, and obscene language. 9 Stop lying

to one another, now that you have taken off the clothes of old nature with your vices, 10...

2 Thessalonians 3: 11-15
11... among you, there are some who are lazy, not working on anything, and who only get into what they don't care about. 12 We command such people and exhort in the Lord Jesus Christ, that they should calmly set out to work for a living. 13 Ye, brethren, do not tire of doing good. 14 If any man does not obey the instructions which we give unto them in this letter, report him publicly, and do not relate to him, that he may be ashamed. 15 Nevertheless, have him not as an enemy, but admonish him as a brother.

1 Timothy 1:9-10
9... the law has not been instituted for the righteous, but for the disobedient and rebellious, for the wicked and sinners, for the irreverent and profane.

The law is for those who mistreat their own parents, for murderers, 10 for adulterers and homosexuals, for slave dealers, liars, and corrupt.

In short, the law is for all that is against sound doctrine.
1 Timothy 3: 1-16

1..., if any man wishes to be a bishop,... 2... the bishop must be unimpeachable, husband of one woman, moderate, sensible, respectable, hospitable, able to teach; 3 He must not be drunk or slang, nor a friend of money, but kind and gentle. 4 He must govern his house well, and have his children obey him with all due respect; 5 For he that cannot govern his own family, how can he take care of the church of God? 6 It should not be a newly converted, let alone become presumptuous and fall into the same condemnation in which the devil fell. 7 It is also required that those who do not belong to the church speak well of him, that they may not fall into discredit and in the trap of the devil. 8 The deacons, too, must be honorable, sincere, not friends of the much wine, not greedy of the ill-gotten gains. 9 They must keep, with a clean conscience, the great truths of faith. 10 Let them first be put to the test, and then, if there is nothing to reproach them, that they may serve as deacons. 11 Likewise, the wives of deacons must be honorable, not slanderous, but moderate and worthy of trust. 12 The deacon must be the husband of one woman, and rule his children well, and his own house. 13 Those who exercise the diaconate will gain a place of honor and gain greater confidence to speak of their faith in Christ Jesus. 14..., 15... 16 There is no doubt that the mystery of our faith is great

1 Timothy 5: 11-15

11... younger widows,... when their passions drive them away from Christ, he gives them to marry. 12 Thus they are guilty of failing their first commitment. 13 In addition, they are accustomed to being idle and walking from house to house. And they not only become lazy but also gossipy and meddling, talking about what they shouldn't. 14 Wherefore I urge young widows to marry and have children, and to bring their homes well, and to give no place for criticism of the enemy. 15 And it is that some have already gone astray to follow Satan.

1 Timothy 6: 7-10
7 For we brought nothing into this world, and we can bring nothing away. 8 So if we have clothes and food, let us be content with that. 9 Those who desire to be enriched fall into temptation, and become slaves to their many desires. These unknowable and damaging plunge people into ruin and destruction. 10 For the love of money is the root of all kinds of evils. To covet it, some have deviated from the faith and caused a lot of disappointment.

1 Timothy 6: 17-19
17 To the rich of this world, let them not be arrogant, nor put their hope in riches,... 18 Tell them that they do good, that they may be rich in good works, and generous, ready to share what they have. 19 In this way, they shall treasure for themselves a sure flow for the future, and they shall obtain true life.
2 Timothy 2: 22-26

22 Flee from the evil passions of youth, and try to follow righteousness, faith, love, and peace, together with those who call upon the Lord with a clean heart. 23 Have nothing to do with foolish and meaningless arguments, for you know that they end up in disputes. 24 And a servant of the Lord must not walk in a fight; rather, he should be kind to everyone, able to teach and not prone to irritation. 25 Thus, humbly, he must correct the adversaries, in the hope that God will grant them repentance to know the truth, 26 that they may wake up and escape from the trap in which the devil holds them captive, submissive to his will.

2 Timothy 3: 1-9

1... difficult times will come in the last few days. 2 People shall be full of selfishness and greed; they will be boastful, arrogant, blasphemers, disobedient to parents, ungrateful, ungodly, 3 callous, relentless, slanderous, libertine, ruthless, enemies of all that is good, 4 treacherous, impetuous, vain and more friends of pleasure than of God. 5 They shall appear to be pious, but their conduct shall deny the power of piety. With those people, don't even mess with them! 6 Thus are they that go from house to house, captivating weak women laden with sins, who let themselves be carried away with all kinds of passions. 7 They are always learning, but they never know the truth. 8 Just as Janes and Jambres opposed Moses, they also oppose the truth. They are depraved-minded people, reproved in faith. 9 But they shall not go far, for all the world shall realize his foolishness, as they did with those two.

Tito 3: 1-3

DEPRESSION **doomed**

1 Remind them all that they must be obedient and subscribed to the rulers and the authorities. They must always be willing to do good: 2 not to speak ill of anyone, but to seek peace and be respectful, demonstrating full humility in their dealings with everyone. 3 In another time we too were foolish and disobedient. We were wayward and were slaves of all kinds of passions and pleasures. We lived in malice and envy. We were loathsome and we hate each other.

Within the Bible, you can find more precepts that tell us what God's will is, but with this is more than enough to realize and understand what we should consider as "right" which should always be equivalent to standards with what d let's compare ourselves to be "normal."

All this is considered as "Moral Law" and we must fulfill it if we one day yearn to have a place in heaven, however this "law" that should be known, accepted and obeyed at least by those who claim to be Christians, is not observed by the majority of Christians and non-Christians because "penalty" or "punishment" for them for break it does not represent "anything serious or realistic"... for those who want to fulfill it as much as they can and those who do not simply ignore it... they are in the mercy of God.

However, world society wants to feel protected, and so the "legal laws" and "social laws" emerged.

In addition to what has already been pointed out, countless descriptions of what is "normal, correct, adequate, wise or reasonable" can be found and perhaps many other synonyms, however, there are certain situations in which it might not be so easy to determine whether or not it is". normal,"

For example:

- Is it normal to study for so many years?
- Is it normal to get married too young?
- Is it normal to live alone?
- Is it normal for poverty and hunger?
- Is it normal to paint everything blue?
- Is it normal for cars to be very large?
- Is it normal for trees to be in a city?
- Is it normal for a man to have much power?
- Is it normal to hate someone who offended me?
- Etcétera.

Whether it is normal at first sight, we must bear in mind that we must use our most healthy judgment in order to evaluate, and if necessary, consult with someone with experience and maturity, we must bend the "ego" and give way to humility.

There is much written about it and I have noticed that throughout the world there are different criteria about what is "normal", either according to their laws or according to their religions and I think that

any of those versions could be accepted as true...
adding that "the normal" is expressed not only in
positive affirmations or direct commandments but
also with prohibitions of what should not be done.

However, even though the Bible contains tragic
stories and prophecies that many of us would not
want to be fulfilled, it also contains the wisdom of
men inspired by God our creator and that is why it
must be the standard for measuring what is
"normal."

This must be our starting point so that after
comparing ourselves honestly we know where we
will have to go if we want to live in peace and
harmony.

What the Bible describes and establishes may have
overlap slays with the religion and philosophy of
other peoples and cultures, since its content includes
universal values that make us common to all human
beings, particularl…, the right to life.

Those who belong to other religions or who claim
not to be religious may or may not accept what this
book proposes, that is, they will be able to explain
in their way of suffering and how it can be
overcome. and if they wish, they will also be able to
review other sources of information, and where they
will surely find significant similarities of scientific
or spiritual aspects mentioned or explained in this
book.

Item 13

Science and faith connexion

In appearance, science does not admit the power of faith, and faith does not recognize the achievements and scopes of science.

At one point it could be said that both sources do not need each other but, it seems that the two ignore that neither would be useful if they did not have the power of "The Mind" that is the one that knows of both and can produce successful or disastrous results.

The pillars of science have been observation and methodology, while for faith, history and mystery have been.

Faith is much older than science and although it has gone its own way, in many ways it ends up reaching the site of faith.

And although I already explain it in chapter 6, here I want to show again in this synoptic picture the meaning, scope, and essence of "the mind"
See the chart on the next page

Soul:	The divine spark, the energy that gives life.
Spirit:	The "implant" in the heart made by God containing information that guides our actions according to his will (Spiritual Body – Holy Spirit)
Mind:	The action that occurs simultaneously by the interaction of the soul and the spirit, making decisions that materialize in thoughts that in turn provoke reactions in the brain
Brain:	The physical part of the body that synchronizes movements, actions, and reactions of an emotional or spiritual physical nature.

Then and for that reason, the goal of this book is:

***To help people who suffer physically, emotionally
or socially, find the best way to alleviate
their grief, to recover or to learn to cope it
to live with dignity and also to learn to
achieve the best version of themselves.***

This goal is somehow the same as science and faith have been proposed, the latter through God, church, and religion.

And the same has been attempted by countless other people and institutions.

We're all trying, we'd all like to do it for everyone's good.

People with "mental" illnesses and certain physical illnesses... like the other sick people "the normal ones"... are seeking for help and want to be healed.

We have all come the same way to regaining health; maybe after we've applied Grandma's "recipes" first we went to the family doctor and from there we were able to look for any other means no matter what, for the sole purpose of being and feeling good physically and emotionally.

A person is considered sick when they are outside the parameters that may regard them as normal physically, emotionally and socially.

But there are diseases that can be barbed or make that person a cripple; generally the "body" is healthy and can be altered by different factors of which viruses and bacteria are the most dangerous on a physical level because they can damage the vital organs of the person.

It can also be said that a person is "sick" when he has the flu or when an external event caused him to burn, cut or fracture of his body, in which case only good care and time will be required for the body itself to heal with its own resources.

Now, speaking of the most popular "mental illnesses" such as anxiety, depression or bipolarity... it is not so easy to determine the cause even though science has advanced in leaps and bounds. some attribute the cause to a dysfunctional nest of the genetic origin of the brain, which makes the disease a "physical" and not "mental" problem.

This means that a person may suffer a "chemical imbalance" due to social problems (external factors) that affect his emotions causing the poor function of the hormone-producing glands such as Serotonin, Melatonin or any other.

In this field, the advances of science have been intended to "level" the functioning of these glands through "pills" sometimes achieving some well-being in the patient, although this well-being is usually temporary.

Others say the problem is "mental" but they haven't tried it because they themselves haven't agreed to define "the mind."

However, science through psychology has considered that therapy (listening and giving ideas or good advice, and even noting some flaw in the perception of reality) can help the individual restore their "mental" health

This type of therapy treatment is very good without a doubt, but it is only part of the solution besides that by itself (the therapy) presents limitations due to its application so spaced, because usually the therapist meets with the patient once a week although at difficult cases they come to meet more frequently and thus manage to "calm" the patient by making him see his "problem" less serious or less threatening.

That's how science has been treating these kinds of "mental illnesses.

It is surprising, however, that psychology has not realized that changing or correcting a patient's behavior... it's equivalent to teaching him a new language... And a new language is only learned and mastered through permanent practice... In other words, and in my own way, it means replacing and installing new "mental implants."

I would very much like psychology to consider this message as a contribution on my part to adjust their therapeutic techniques and procedures.
But who knows how many of those people who have received therapy have truly healed?

Some statistics speak of percentages or amounts, for example, 5% of adolescents or 1 in 5... the truth is that there are no reliable statistics that can tell us how many people have suffered from these mental illnesses, how many have died because of it or how many have recovered.

Today, in the world according to the most recent data from the UN (2017), the CIA (2017) and the real-time population clock Census.gov, it can be estimated that there are currently some 7.5 billion people in the world (the year 2019).

A patient can heal when he believes that what they are giving or doing is good for him, that is when he is fully convinced...

That conviction is FE, yet it is not only faith in God or science but can be a mixture, for each patient possesses different information (mental implants) that can be found in the depths of his being (in the subconscious).

And so, when this patient "remembers" a successful event where some acquaintance received some treatment then believes that with him it will work the same and especially when the person who does the treatment enjoys fame, prestige, and good reputation... and if you are also a believer in any religion, you will have greater opportunities to heal because you will be convinced that God will guide the hand of one who will heal you.

Thus, it is how the connection between science and faith happens.

Such is the case for patients who are given placebos (medicines without active chemical content) and say that the drug worked very well for them... even without knowing that what he was prescribed was a placebo... and it works because "the mind" or "the brain" collaborates to make that happen, because of some "mental implant"

Words can also be "placebos" and even surgery... the important thing is that the patient believes that what they are doing to him and that whoever does it deserves their respect and trust.

Whether it is physical or mental illness, the patient will heal if he is convinced that what they will do to him will work... so that part of the recovery process is precisely the renewal of the mind.

This is how science and faith operate. that's the connection.

The essential elements for renewing the mind are new mental implants, faith, and love.... And of course "Targeted Introspection"

Item 14

Mind Renewing

To understand the meaning of "renewing the mind" I allowed myself to bring to case 2 examples that may cause as much surprise as others to whom I have given the seminar.

First:
In my book "A New God," I define God as follows:

An Ineffable Mystery
knowing its essence and seeing his work
we can create him with imagination
we can interpret his will and the path forward

Second:
Also in my book, I said that the Spaniards had come to Latin America by mistake as they planned to go to the lands of India... and that they had come to impose on the indigenous people a new God.

But as I reviewed a little more the background of the coming of the Spaniards, I found something that caught my attention and from there came a new "inspiration" that justifies or ties my intellect with spirituality (science with faith).

After further analysis, the point reaches the next consideration"
The Spaniards or anyone else came to Latin America to impose on a new God, that was not their original purpose but to bring the gospel, without a doubt nevertheless "finding" treasures became their priority; the issue was made up of people who no one would miss if they ever died.

Chances are, these people didn't know the gospel beyond what they were told to say. and what they said to the natives was that they should know God, not knowing that they, according to their prophecies, were waiting for the arrival of a new God.

The natives believed that the God they were talking about was the same God they were expecting influenced by the visit of the Vikings from more than 300 years ago.

The image they had of the God who would come dressed in European armor like the Vikings whom they had known.

The Spaniards should have taught the gospel as the Kings had entrusted to Torcuato Luca de Tena (inquisitor of the new Spain) who after the Muslims had been expelled from their land, established the rules for doing so.

And so they did, bringing the "good news" by letting them know that:

- There was a better world (the kingdom of God) to which those who repented of their sins could aspire (of evil acts committed against oneself and others)

- Whenever they agree to live according to the teachings of "Jesus" (love your neighbor, do not do to others what you do not want for you).

A message that the natives accepted thinking that their prophecies were being fulfilled.

Seen in this way, we can realize that they did not come to tell us what God was like but who he was, for they did not know it themselves as the Bible itself says in John 1: 18 "No one ever saw Him..."

Then, what the Spaniards came to, was to **"re-educate"** the indigenous because they found them savages because of their nudity... and they wanted them to learn to behave according to God's will through Christ Jesus.

What's important about all this is that you know that when you communicate with God whatever you call him, what you're doing is expressing your words, desires and feelings from the bottom of your heart

thinking of an almighty being you can trust and for whom you can still trust hope for a better world.
You may agree with my reflections or perhaps not but I did it during my search for the truth. So, my way of thinking changed because I made my knowledge, I came to the purest conviction and decided that if there is no one I hurt I can go on like this... with the enviable ability to feel an intimate relationship with God, the Almighty.

In the same way, you can also reflect on everything you know about life and create your own version until you convince yourself and act accordingly, without forgetting that you must adhere to the "Law" so as not to harm third people and live in peace.

Well, that's what **re-educate** is all about, that's what updating your false old beliefs is all about, updating your thinking.

Therefore, instead of saying "renew the mind", we should say **"re-educate the mind"**, because as explained in chapter "5", this is not a material object like a piece of furniture, a building or a car that over time loses its beauty and functionality and only suffices with change the damaged parts so that they look like new again and continue to work.

We know "the mind" is an abstract concept that is used to describe the process of thought.

Holy Spirit implanted by God in our hearts

More:
Meaning of perception of external

Factors through the 5 senses

Equal to:

Thoughts that generate beliefs

Thought: is the faculty, action, and effect of thinking. The thought is also an idea or mental representation about something or someone perceived through the senses.

Then the thoughts are received and interpreted by the brain, which in turn sends instructions to the body and the body reacts according to the instructions received.

Reactions are those that give identity to the person concerned as he behaves according to the content of the message received.

Each time this whole process is carried out, the brain collects and archives all kinds of information according to the cultural environment of the individual.

That information is used by the brain whenever it needs to make a decision to send instructions to any part of the body.

So what we must understand is that the individual whom everyone can see is the one who manifests the instructions taken by the brain according to the information he has been accumulating throughout the life of the individual.

Any type of information that each person receives is what is shaping their education and with it over time, many of their reactions become automatic since by constantly repeating the instructions learned they become "habit", same that facilitates the individual's response more immediately.

Habit: This word refers to a special way of proceeding, acquired by incidence or repetition of similar and equal acts, as a custom or a practice originated by an intrinsic trend, is an action that someone performs so many times that "it becomes habit," and habits can become mania, and even obsessions in certain cases.

From a psychological point of view, the human being is able to get used to action, to the point of needing it to be well with himself.

For example, when someone who works in an office is going to spend a long vacation out of town, a strange week drinking coffee at their desk, because for that person, it has been part of their daily routine of work and other functions for many years
When a person changes an object or routine to which he or she is used to using or repeating, he will automatically feel discomfort with the new, since what he replaces, adapted to his needs and tastes.

When the human being feels comfortable, he will have no interest in continuing to enjoy that comfort.

When it comes to effective habits, for example, if one person is comfortable with another, feelings will be born to the extent that they will share the time available, it will become a habit to live with that person.

The same goes for moral habits, human behavior is based on principles based on society, doing good or doing evil, it can become a common thing without any problem.

A person's identity (what we see, know or know about him/her), regardless of age, is the result of the education he or she receives in his/her social and cultural environment.

The most important information in his life (mental implants) is received in the first 6 years of age when after learning the language, he has also been able to learn the main patterns of behavior and communication.

So the only way to "re-educate the mind" is to "re-educate the individual," that is, by providing information that conforms to the standards of legal, social and moral laws.

And this is not so simple because it is equivalent to teaching you a new language, which means that as you get older, the greater the degree of difficulty in learning the communication patterns of the new language.

When a child who already speaks a language is taken to a country where another language is spoken and enlisted in school, he listens daily and practices that new language and very soon masters it... but if it is an adult who does not attend school daily or practices constantly, then the learning process can take a long, a long time and may never master the new language... However, you will learn at least the most essential skills to communicate... and finally, it will all depend on the intensity with which you participate and the effort spent to achieve it.

To educate is to give, provide, transfer knowledge, that is, the information acquired by others (mainly our predecessors) who have acquired it through experimentation.

Imagine the implant in the soil of seed from an apple tree... when it grows it will bear fruit i.e. the apple that developed with the inherent genetic codes.

The same goes for human beings... What he hears and what he sees, accompanied by an explanation or description, is what is equivalent to the seed that is planted in the earth and therefore, just as when the individual grows will necessarily bear fruit that will be nothing more than what was implanted (sown) in his mind...

The tree will never bear any fruit other than the apple... unless the seed is intentionally or accidentally altered, as has already happened in fruits, plants, and animals.

Thus, man can "alter" the information with which he grew up... and knowing the standards of information, it's all a matter of "sowing" it as if it were a new seed that will alter or correct for the better the information it received since it was born.

As the human being grows, he is using the information that he has received and that is updated over time, by cultural interaction and by coexistence with the community.

The most useful information to live with the community is retained in the conscious and the least common or important goes to the subconscious.

Therefore, and according to what I have researched, to offer real help to the people who suffer (some know it, others admit it and others do not, and many others ignore it), it is necessary that several elements be coincident.
Out of my own curiosity, I began to investigate why the churches are trying to help heal people and I could see that in addition to relying on the Bible (John 14:12)

"Indeed, indeed, I say unto you, He that believeth in me, the works which I do also he shall do; and greater than these will do; because I go to Father",...

They have also relied on being able to do so, implementing what some authors have written about motivation, leadership, self-help and psychological techniques, however, there has not been much that they have achieved because what they have done has been rather informative.

In my search I met several techniques and methods that led me to believe that well understood and applied correctly could give magnificent results in the process of the renewal of the mind, so I gave myself the task of merging some parts of those techniques and methods by adding the main ingredient that is the "Faith with Science".

DEPRESSION **doomed**

My conclusions led me to a theory that has become a method, and is to add in the equation the concept and understanding of "the mind" in such a way that it leaves no doubt about what should be understood as such, for as from the beginning I have emphasized, people are very much given to making a misuse of language and that generates significant flaws in communication.

In addition, the proposal of this method includes its practical application so that it does not remain alone in a course or seminar more like all the ones I have known, where they tell us how it could be better but everything is left at the theory level.

This method, unlike others, has as a priority (at least) to offer participants the elements that allow them to continue to build the best version of themselves.

I called this method:

"TARGETED INTROSPECTION""

And it will be held in the workshop that will be taught constantly and that will be periodically informed on:
https://humanintrospection.wixsite.com/website
or www.mariosinlimites.com
Also asking for information at:
mario.sinlimites@yahoo.com

TARGETED INTROSPECTION

The self-healing workshop

INSTRUCTOR'S GUIDE

I
GENERAL VISION

The instructor should explain correctly and totally the content of the author's book "DEPRESSION DOOMED" theme by theme and connect it with the "participants guide" for them to learn and assimilate the method to be developed to get better results.

1. Objective

The challenge and goal is to instill in the participant sufficient confidence that in an environment of security and confidentiality at the conclusion of the conference and the self-healing workshop of "Targeted Introspection" will be able to achieve any of the 3 objectives that we're chasing for help people who suffer physically, emotionally or socially due to stress, anxiety or depressive to:

1. Full recovery
2. Stabilize to find the best way to ease your grief, and live with dignity
3. Learn how to build the best version of yourself recovering or not.

2. About the self-healing workshop

As the workshop requires psychological and theological management, it is necessary to develop it in the following order:

1. Having thoughtfully read the book 'DEPRESSION doomed' and agreeing with its contents

2. Explain the basics of the seminar and the self-healing workshop; that is, to speak to the participant of the experiences experienced by the author in the quest to relieve the pain caused by depression.

3. Talk about most other methods that do not work because they are not applied correctly due to:

   a. Not enough time is spent and they do not deal with the issue deeply

   b. The participant does not clearly understand what his achievement will be

   c. Exponents do not have enough information

   d. The institutions or persons who deliver it do not do so as to prime but as a secondary service

   e. Confusing language is used

   f. No follow-up, the participant goes home and it's all over

4. Show the participant the source of what should be considered normal, according to the Bible and

other sacred or scientific books... I mean the comparison standard

5. Permanently teach (to the point of exhaustion) positive statements contained in the Bible where they can be recognized and accepted as a child of God and realize that as they are, they are perfect and they can improve or correct any situation in their lives.

6. Explain what "introspection" is by reviewing the definition of the word in item 4 "the same language" in the book "Depression doomed" as well as how it should be done in accordance with the participant's guide.

II

THE SELF-HEALING WORKSHOP

1. Universe Creation

Start by the creation of the universe and standardize knowledge about who or what is God and what is good and bad.

Explain the essence of and what God's will would be, and how the human being thinking about it and by divine inspiration has been able to write down the Bible and other sacred or scientific books throughout history.

The author in his book "A New God", describes the concept of God as follows:

"It's an ineffable mystery

Knowing its essence and seeing his work

We can create it with our imagination

Interpret its will and know the way to follow"

2. Human Body… the brain

Talk about the human body functioning, particularly of the brain.

At this point, the facilitator can rely on a video display, drawings on the board, or any other means that allow him/her to clearly explain that the brain itself does not emit signals or instructions to the rest of the body unless it has received information processing and has prosecuted it by interpreting its meaning.

3. Good, bad, normal, abnormal

Differentiate the good from the bad, the normal from the abnormal.

Explain how false beliefs are discovered, how they affect and how knowledge of the truth can become to be.

4. Reliability of the Biblia and other Books

Here, it must be explained that what we call divine inspiration is the product of the awakening of consciousness, it is to realize and interpret the facts and experiences, to say what God's will would be for his creation to endure and transcend.

It is the interpretation of God's will embodied in writing in the Bible and other sacred books so that we all have access to his knowledge and can study and analyze it to adhere to the truth.

They are evolutionary writings that are updated by thinkers around the world pursuing the same goal of preserving the human race.

5. Different ways for faith

Explain why according to the different cultures of the world there are different forms of faith and why they can all work positively

The human being who originally appeared in ancient Mesopotamia as they seek better living conditions (climate, food, house) was emigrated in groups and spread throughout the world on different continents.

The different groups lived their own experiences by confronting the rigors of nature and discovering the natural phenomena to decide where to settle themselves and then began to seek the origin of their presence in the universe.

That is why each group generates its own convictions and in one way or another everyone understands that there is a superior being to them, and since then they refer to that being with different names and perform rituals to venerate and thank them for what they consider they receive from "heaven" or from the afterlife.

Thus, people's community grow, and as we all know they struggled to possess greater territories and fighting by power began, and obviously the victors imposed their beliefs and lifestyles on the vanquished.

However, what we must keep in mind is that regardless of how each group perceived the higher power, all identify God as a powerful being to which no human being can equate.

Therefore, they all turn to that higher being to ask, to offer and worship him.

Then, the intention that arises from the hearth of every human being on the planet is exactly the same no matter the place on earth where it comes from.

I mean... everyone is right and the truth is for him or her.

However, everyone expresses it differently.

6. Parallels or similarities of healing, between the Bible and Science.

Explain the parallels or similarities of recovery between the Bible and Science.

The Bible speaks of the suffering of mankind and attributes it to sins, but it also offers ways to make amends and find the right path.
Science also knows about human suffering and although it has mostly focused on the physical part, it has also

discovered that there is a non-physical part that can influence its malfunction.

The Bible indicates that to stop suffering we must change our way of thinking that it is supposed to be contaminated by deception and lies, to begin to think of the terms of God's will.

Science discovers that many diseases come from the wrong way to care for our bodies, and is attributed to the way we live, which means the way we act and act according to the way of thinking that we have received throughout our lives.

In addition, science has found a way to help people to discover their personality and realize whether or not it is necessary to modify their behavior and how to do it.

7. Most common causes of suffering... influence on personality

Talk of the most common causes of suffering and how it influences personality.

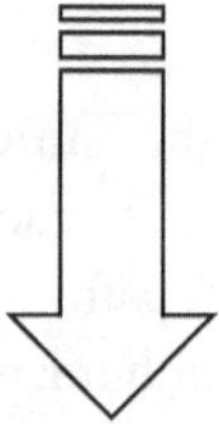

DEPRESSION **doomed**

"Normal People"	Causes of alteration of personality	"Abnormal People"
Physically and emotionally healthy	**IN CHILDHOOD** Physical, verbal, emotional or psychologic parents' mistreat.	Physically and emotionally sick
Energetics		Tired, exhausted
Enthusiasts	Sexual abuse	Shany, Apathetic
Sociables	Abandon	Loneliness
Optimists	Bully, humiliations	Pessimists
Happy and Funny	Extreme poverty	Very serious and very formals
Focused	**IN ADOLESCENCE**	Lack of attention
Good self-esteem	Bully, humiliations	Low self-esteem
Trusty	Bad fella	
Good children	Drugs, alcohol	Untrusty, Jealousy Envies
Good Parents	Bad sexual experiences	Bad children
Good spouses	Misinformation	Very strict an authority parents
Good workers	**IN ADULTHOOD**	Comptroller parents
Good friends	Bully, Humiliations at work	Gossipy, Lasy, Boycotters Workers
Etcétera	Romanticly rejected	
	Cheating	
	Lies	
	Work failures	Cannot be good friends
	Broken marriage	
	Misinformation	Etcétera

8. Failures and causes in life

Teach participants how to identify life failures and identify the causes

When the concept of good and evil is already clear, and what we must consider right for having a standard starting point, then, according to the biblical precepts, "introspection" should be made generally based on terms of morality.

Introspection should contain the aspects that are often most relevant to any human being, for example:

- Relationship with parents

- Behavior with friends

- Behavior with friends

- Job performance

- Marital coexistence

- Dealing with children

- Sources of wealth

- Etcetera.

Discuss with participants what would be normal or correct within each of these lines so that they can recognize where there was an event or situation that had deviated or gone from the right

9. How the thoughts work in the brain

Explain how thoughts act in the brain and how psychosomatic diseases can be triggered.

By saying that the brain controls the body doesn't mean the brain alone gives instructions to each part of the body to act in a certain way.

The brain controls the body by monitoring its functions, that is, the brain was gradually identifying the structure and chemical composition of each part of our body and thus classifying them as "normal", so when something happens outside of the expected or already been recorded by the brain, it reacts to indicate that something is not working properly.

For example, the skin perceives different sensations during the day that are familiar to the brain but if it receives a prick, that is unfamiliar and then the brain "turns on" the alarm giving the coordinates to locate where is happening something unusual in the body and we can review it immediately.

With the information we obtain, the brain concludes whether everything goes well or determines the degree of damage and as a result communicates with other parts of the body to prevent and safeguard its integrity; if all is well, the brain returns to its resting state and the alert is removed, tolerating the awkward moment that the external agent might generate.

10. Who we are physically, socially and spiritually.

To help the participants to identify their real position in life, we must talk to them about the different economic levels, social positions, job positions, standards of beauty and health, as well as spirituality... They must be very clear who is who.

11. Use our strength or let it to God

Help identify strengths and how to use them to feel better, how far to leave it to God and from where it is dedicated to acting on the participant and how to do so

Give them tools to discover that they are good and that they are bad or very bad, they must understand what strengths mean, because often it is only measured by economic power and not by what they can actually do according to their knowledge , skills, physical abilities, etcetera, to make what it takes to be better at what has been given to them by God, and to make them understand that the gifts they have received should be exercised and not to confuse that God will always do for them what they ask for.

Teach them to recognize the possibilities at their disposal to heal or learn to live with their reality when it cannot be modified.

12. Healing chances or learning to cope with reality.

Since they have understood their real position and situation in life, they must realize that to help themselves they have done little or almost nothing, they have always let someone else help them.

So, teach them to research for themselves what opportunities they have with advances in science, understanding cost and opportunity.

13. Small groups participation

Engage them in small groups to speak openly, honestly and sincerely about their suffering and accept the opinion or advice they may receive from their peers.

After the participant self-evaluation, he/she must decide if he/she finds it objective, reasonable and achievable

Explaining how the facilitator will initiate the topics that need to be addressed to help them get to know each other better, so that they discover the real reason for where their suffering may come from, highlighting them that it is about making someone else be aware of the results of moral personal introspection to include:

• Sex, from the first time you knew about it, and all the experiences lived up to this day, understanding that the most important thing is to detect whether sex has been a positive or negative factor in their lives as well as to discover the feelings and thoughts that have a nest.

This point should include how their relationships have been, recognizing the most significant, and if the relationship ended, how this happened?

• The family environment from birth to current age, identifying their position within the whole family and whether their family likes them or not and why, including treatment with parents, siblings, cousins, uncles, grandparents, and family friends

• Professional experience and job performance from the first job to present, talking about their achievements or failures as well as their expectations for the future.

• School life from kindergarten to the most advanced level studied or continuing to study, as well as discover whether you are preparing for something they truly like or perhaps are doing just to please family or friendly desires.
• Review the 7 deadly sins and develop a summary of those the instructor thinks to need more understanding or support.

14.   To know and trust in Gods' word

Teach them to know and trust in the word of God and seek to live in harmony with their community

Teach them how to look in the Bible for a particular topic or point where they can find hope that things will be better.

15. Mental Re-implants

Talk to them about the model of mental re-implants.

Briefly explain to them that it might consist of some models such as Dr. Leaf's 21-day technique or positive affirmation technique or creative visualization technique, or the 4 simple steps of Ho'oponopono.... Or a combination of these and some others according to the information obtained

.

16. Design the best version of themselves.

Once the workshop is over, having a clear awareness of their false beliefs and having identified their current problems and their origin and without fear having confronted old ghosts (memories), they will objectively have to develop a plan to achieve their personal goal with which they are convinced to achieve it and accept it as their new way of life, beginning to behave as best they can through good intentions and good deeds.

TARGETED INTROSPECTION

The self-healing workshop

PARTICIPANT'S GUIDE

PARTICIPANT'S GUIDE

1. Attend the "Targeted Introspection" seminar and the "Self-Healing Workshop", and make sure you have understood all the content exposed by the speaker or instructor and have any questions you deem necessary to know how you will achieve the renewal of your mind and how you will be able to work on the construction of the best version of yourself.

2. One of the main objectives of the "workshop" is that you know how to perform a deep and serious introspection of your life so that you discover and highlight your faults and successes, always keeping in mind that the objective of this introspection will be to identify the weakness and strengths of your personality, as well as what have been the factors that most influenced your current personality.

For example, you should determine if you are Aggressive, Shy, Introverted, Sociable, Daring, Prudent, etc... that is, all those characteristics that you consider to be part of you.

3. Introspection should contain the most relevant aspects of your life, without omitting anything because it causes embarrassment, mortification or fear. Asking yourself, "What's the most serious

thing I've ever done to somebody else? And what's the most serious thing they've ever done to me? it can help you remember some details you might want never to know but to heal you need to be courage and determined to face your ghosts.

Introspection can be done as a story in chronological order from birth to today, or it can be done in specific stages of life from 0 to 5 years, from 6 to 12, from 13 to 20 etcetera.

But for the purposes of this method, it is highly recommended that no matter which model you prefer, you should include the most important "areas" in a person's life for example:

• "Area 1" The Family

• "Area 2" Love (including sexuality)

• "Area 3" Profession and job performance

• "Area 4" Social Position

• "Area 5" Economic Position

• "Area 6" Physical and mental health

• "Area 7" Religion and Spiritual Health

4. Make a list derived from your introspection, from the situations or events that with their possible

negative or even positive consequences may have contributed to generating the "tribulations of your personality".

You can follow the example of **"Table A"**

5. The result of introspection helps the participant to remember events of great importance in his life and allows to have a very clear awareness of the events that could affect him physically and emotionally. It is therefore highly recommended to review with the instructor on the outstanding aspects to develop an action plan that initiates the process of change or adjustment.

6. After responsibly complying with the above points and understanding that you have acquired a great knowledge of yourself and the universe around you, you should be able to know what may be the best version you can build of yourself and you will have the support of the instructor to help you prepare a plan to achieve it.

In the end, the instructor will provide a self-assessment sheet where the participant will determine and decide whether he or she might require further support to determine their recurrence.

INTROSPECTION ÁREAS
"ÁREA 1"
Family

Many times, and without us noticing, one of the main causes of disquiet can be in the family... I'm sure we've all heard about "sleeping with the enemy".

However, due to the daily coexistence, we suddenly stopped realizing that this coexistence has become routinary and that the way we treat each other is normal.

We get used to screaming, disorder, and many other behaviors that, far from the family feeling calm and happy, they feel stressed, sad or angry.

But, to what degree is it normal for any of the members to feel uncomfortable?

That is why it is very important to know to whom we recognize as members of our family and to know what our position is within it and how is our relationship with each of the members, for example:

1. Who is the highest member of the family, the leader?

2. Do I admire and respect the authority of the family leader?

3. Do I know the values, dreams, achievements, ideals of the family?, do I agree with that?

4. Would I like someone else to take the lead instead?

5. Do I think I'm better treated than my brothers or sisters?

6. I don't think anyone takes care of me?

7. Do I feel that my parents have a preference for someone other than me?

8. Do I feel that all family members respect me, appreciate me, trust me, support me, show me their affection?

9. Do they always take my opinion on important matters?

10. Are men better than women?

11. How is the relationship of my family with other family members such as uncles, grandparents, cousins, nephews?

12. Do we help each other among all family members?

13. Are there family secrets we wouldn't want others to know?

"AREA 2"
Love (including sexuality)

Being accepted or rejected by one or more people definitely influences our personality, and depending on our beliefs, influence can be great or fatal.

Considering ourselves good lovers, elevate or maintain our self-esteem and make us feel confident that we will have no trouble choosing or finding our true love, our life partner, with whom we will be happy.

However, it is very important to know that we have been able to discover our false beliefs and that we have reasonable assurance that we are not being deceived or judged ourselves on our situation from the wrong perspective.

Just also it is so important our looking, love, and accepting us as part of God's creation, we should not allow our happiness depends on our appearance or our ability to "conquer" couples.

2.1 Romantic Love:

1. Remembering the first experience of love (without sexual aspects), describing how old you were, who was the one that made you feel that kind of love and how would you describe it, and how this ended up?

2. What were the loving relationships where there was no sexual intercourse? From what age and what kind of memories were left...?

3. If you could go back to some of those old loves, who would be and why?

4. I did not dare speak to somebody, or I was rejected by someone, and what did I feel, and what did I think the reasons could be?

5. Did I always have the easy way to approach the person I liked?

6. I approached all the people I liked or only those I thought would pay attention to me.

7. I always felt "good looking" and knew that I could catch anyone's eye?.

8. I never dared compete for someone, because I knew I was going to lose or because I so prided.

9. Did I say I love you, or what I thought to the person I was interested in as a couple?

2.2 Erotic Love, Sex and Passion:

1. When and how did I first know about sex?

2. Did I think sex was something dirty or sinful?

3. When, how, where and with whom did my first sexual relationship happen?

4. Do I like watching pornography?

5. My sex intercourses have been satisfactory or not and why?

6. Is there a problem or conflict related to my sex life?

7. Do I feel an excessive desire for sex?

8. Have I had problems harassing or being harassed by someone?

9. Do I sexually depend on someone or something?

DEPRESSION **doomed**

"ÁREA 3"

Profession, Social and Economic Position

To me, there are 2 choices each person should take very carefully… choose the profession or trade that he/she would like to perform in his life and choose the right partner.

However, many times even if we start our lives with that vision in mind, fate does its job and gives us great surprises, sometimes it gives us more than we expected and sometimes less.

The important thing here is to always keep in mind that in making our choice, we must do so with all the intensity of our hearts and not fall into the trap of temptation.

1. Do I have the job I like?

2. Why did I choose it?

3. Do I like where I work?

4. Do I like the position I occupy?

5. Am I satisfied with the money that I make?

6. Do I get along with my co-workers?

7. Do I feel comfortable with the relationship I have with my boss, my peers or my subordinates?

8. Do I like the level I occupy socially?

9. Do I count on real friends or would I like to find others?

10. Am I happy with the house I live in?

11. Do I get along with my neighbors?

12. I like to invite and be invited to social gatherings?

13. Do I feel comfortable at any social gathering?

DEPRESSION **doomed**

"ÁREA 4"

Physical and Mental Health

It is very important to be aware of our health, as we are all generally well and occasionally get sick and have small discomforts.

But suddenly that "being well" can change and we can start to have more serious illnesses, and if we get sick we usually stop working as we have been doing usually, and sometimes that causes us problems or we cause them.

There are "treacherous" diseases such as high blood pressure or diabetes, which if not detected in time can cause death.

Even if it may seem like a lie, many diseases start with the "stress" that can cause us real physical diseases or psychosomatic diseases that also become real until the psychological cause goes away.

1. Do I pay much attention to my health?

2. Do I notice when I am physically ill or emotionally?

3. Do I recognize symptoms when I am sick?

4. Do I usually feel in a good mood and with energy?

5. Do I sleep well and awake with enthusiasm?

6. Do I visit the doctor or do I take care of myself?

7. Are my feeding habits the same since I was a child?

8. Have I been overweight for a long time?

9. Have I been losing weight?

10. Do I smoke and drink regularly?

11. When was my last medical checkup?

12. Do I exercise regularly?

"AREA 5"

Spiritual Health and Religion

Spiritual health is also very important for living in harmony. Knowing a religion well and practicing provides us with a feeling of faith and hope, it makes us feel that we are not alone and if something bad happens to us, there will always be a God who protects us.

Practicing a religion induces us to be better people and makes us act according to certain rules that usually avoid problems, makes us more sensitive to the suffering of others and motivates us to be of use.

1. Do I believe in God?
2. Are money, fame, and prestige my God?

3. Do I practice any religion?

4. Do I believe in the Bible or the holy book of my

religion?

5. I regularly attend church, what for?

6. Do I feel good whenever I attend?

7. Are all religions the same?

8. Do I think God works miracles?

9. Have I asked "him" for any miracles?

10. Do I pray frequently?

11. Do I feel at peace?

12. Do I feel abandoned or ignored by God?

13. What do I like most about my religion?

14. Do I help someone else whenever I can?

15. As a parent, do I support myself in my religion to guide my children?

16. As a son, have I respected, loved, and obeyed my parents?

17. When I do business, do I take care that it is not advantageous in a bad way?

18. I'm not interested in religion is not necessary

DEPRESSION **doomed**

"TABLE A"

Example of the analysis to make on aspects that influence on personality tribulations

Age	Fact	POSSIBLE CONSEQUENCE
Not born	My mother had an unwanted or problematic pregnancy	Pre-natal stress
1 to 4 years	I was born into complicated childbirth and started to grow up with a lot of carelessness and in adverse family conditions	Very limited childcare amid adult arguments and violence with many screams that frightened me
5 to 6 years old	My parents argued and talked about divorce	Feelings of doubt without knowing what was going on
7 to 12 years old	My dad has left home and my mother takes care of me but leaves me very alone and very often commissions me with my grandparents who also live with financial problems and limitations	I do not feel welcomed, I feel like an intruder received out of pity, missing my mother and without school use
13 years old	I like to play with my friends and I have a hard time doing homework but I'm almost always grounded	I feel without free and forced to do something I don't like, I feel angry and frustrated
	I'm beginning to realize how my parents are and I don't like the way they treat me or how they behave socially in addition to the most extreme poverty in which we live	I feel angry, embarrassed and I start to think that I have to hide my reality, I don't want anybody to know my parents or where I live or under what conditions
	Cousins and friends start talking to me about sex and induce me to discover moments for which I wasn't ready	I early encounter some facets of pleasure, without adequate information and I feel that my soul is disturbed
14 years old	I start confronting my parents and I want to start being "normal" like other young people my age and I'm	I feel guilty for confronting my parents but at the same time I repudiate them, I don't have the ability to pay enough attention at

	already starting to smoke cigarettes	school
	I make community with relatives of very limited circumstances similar to mine, with those I know alcohol and I begin to receive a tremendously sexist influence	I start to depart from my mother's authority, and I feel remorse and sadness but Prefer it instead of still feeling subdued… both feelings are tremendously painful.
15 years old	Girls start to appear in my world and get my attention	I feel inhibited from starting a healthy friendship because I don't have a "normal" family to support my person, nor do I want my world is discovered.
16 to 17 years old	I happen to get a girlfriend older than me but I like her.	I spend most of my time on the relationship, I feel motivated and excited, I get better at school and without realizing it, gradually I become dependent on it and deciding that I will never let her go on my side
18 years old	The relationship with my girlfriend is becoming intense and we start to get intense intimacy	She is discovering a lot of me and I begin to feel the anguish that she will depart from me and I begin to manipulate and blackmail her emotionally. I'm not willing to lose her.
19 years old	My girlfriend gets pregnant, we got married and I started working	I feel relief leaving my mother and I begin to imagine my life would change completely and I will start to be happy. I feel a great desire never to hear from my parents again.
20 to 26 years old	I continue to study, enter the University to study a profession and the responsibilities begin to appear	I'm not prepared to be head of the family, I don't know how to deal with responsibilities, I feel "scared", people start to notice my immaturity and I don't become aware of it until late.
	I want to know the world, feel free and go out with other girls	I behave totally irresponsible as if I were not married and we start to separate and we constantly return until the divorce and the final separation after Having behaved like a jerk
	I drink very often, I go out with several girls without looking for something formal	I'm beginning to have a great feeling of guilt for turning away from my wife and daughter, I feel desolate and full of fear.

27 years old	I finish my studies and no one accompanies me at my graduation, I keep working and I grow little by little	At the same time, I begin to understand that I abandoned my mother in those moments that she needed me and I drink more and more
Etc	Et cetera	I'm starting to find a good partner and I can't find what I wanted.

SEMINAR SELF EVALUATION FORM

1	Did I understand the purpose of the seminar all too well?
2	I clearly understand what my participation should be able
3	I know very well what work I have to do
4	I know very well what my personal goal is
5	I trust that the seminar together with the self-healing workshop will help me achieve my goal
6	I have a comment to make:
	Participant's Name

Completing this questionnaire will help the instructor or speaker make adjustments or changes that are necessary for your best use

Do it with confidence.

Moreover, thank you for participating.